# THE SORCERERS' STONE

# THE POETRY OF ANGELUS SILESIUS

This series presents the poetry of Johann Angelus Silesius in accessible English for modern readers. Angelus's masterwork was the *Cherubinischer Wandersmann*, a collection of over 1,600 short epigrammatic poems, of which no complete English translation exists. The poems translated in this series present the themes likeliest to appeal to contemporary audiences. Topics include fantasy, spiritual alchemy, romance, life as a heroic quest, and the cosmic drama of God's relationship with the human soul.

# THE SORCERERS' STONE

*Alchemical Poems by Angelus Silesius*

**The Poetry of Angelus Silesius**

Translated and Arranged by
RACHEL A. LOTT

RESOURCE *Publications* • Eugene, Oregon

THE SORCERERS' STONE
Alchemical Poems by Angelus Silesius

The Poetry of Angelus Silesius

Resource Publications
An Imprint of Wipf and Stock Publishers
199 W. 8th Ave., Suite 3
Eugene, OR 97401

www.wipfandstock.com

PAPERBACK ISBN: 978-1-6667-4976-2
HARDCOVER ISBN: 978-1-6667-4977-9
EBOOK ISBN: 978-1-6667-4978-6

09/29/22

# Contents

# Introduction

JOHANN ANGELUS SILESIUS (OR Johann Scheffler, 1624–1677) is well known in the history of Christian devotional writings. He has inspired a range of prominent figures, from the evangelist John Wesley to the philosopher Martin Heidegger, and his insights have been compared to those of far eastern mystics. His main poetry collection, the *Cherubinic Wanderer*, stands as a monument to his breadth of knowledge and his poetic skill. The final version of the *Cherubinic Wanderer* contains more than 1,600 epigrams—short, pithy poems usually just two lines long—on everything from daily life to mystical union with God.

In both scholarly and popular circles alike, Angelus has received most attention for his mysticism. Fewer readers realize that Angelus's poetry is also full of fantasy. The phoenix and dragon and basilisk all make appearances, as does the so-called sorcerers' stone or philosophers' stone. But Angelus was not a fantasy writer. He was a realist in an age of dragonish violence, and he wrote his poetry as a guide to the hardest of real-life quests: the transformation of one's own soul into the image of God.

Angelus's *Cherubinic Wanderer* was published just after the religious wars of the seventeenth century.[1] Angelus himself converted from one stripe on the religious spectrum to another, and the conversion was so dramatic that he changed his name. Baptized as Johann Scheffler by Lutheran parents, he later converted to Roman Catholicism and adopted the name Johann Angelus (John the Angel

---

1. For a short overview of Angelus's life and works, see Sammons, "Johann Scheffler."

or Messenger), adding Silesius for his birthplace in Silesia (Poland). Angelus's goal in writing the *Cherubinic Wanderer* was to turn his readers into better Christians, a process he compared to changing lead into gold. Soul-changing is enormously complicated. Angelus describes it variously as an alchemical transmutation, a quest from hell to heaven, a bride preparing for her true love, a castle under siege, an epic battle with dragons and devils, and a mystical union with God. The poems presented in this volume focus on Angelus's alchemical imagery, as well as what lies behind this imagery: a consistent view of wisdom and its role in transforming the soul.

Angelus was not alone in his use of alchemical imagery for theological ends. The great reformer Martin Luther himself, a century earlier, had spoken approvingly of the parallels between alchemy and the Christian doctrine of resurrection:

> The science of alchemy I like well, and, indeed, 'tis the philosophy of the ancients. I like it not only for the profits it brings in melting metals, in decocting, preparing, extracting, and distilling herbs, roots; I like it also for the sake of the allegory and secret signification, which is exceedingly fine, touching the resurrection of the dead at the last day. For, as in a furnace the fire extracts and separates from a substance the other portions, and carries upward the spirit, the life, the sap, the strength, while the unclean matter, the dregs, remain at the bottom, like a dead and worthless carcass; even so God, at the day of judgment, will separate all things through fire, the righteous from the ungodly. The Christians and righteous shall ascend upward into heaven, and there live everlastingly, but the wicked and the ungodly, as the dross and filth, shall remain in hell.[2]

Angelus, like Luther, was alive to the realities of heaven and hell, not as artificial rewards but as the natural result of two opposing processes. The human soul could become either pure or corrupt. To escape its own internal corruption, the soul needed to reverse course and become good; but it could not do this on its own. The transformation required intervention from God. Angelus

2. *The Table Talk of Martin Luther*, 760.

symbolizes this intervention with the paramount alchemical object of his day: the sorcerers' stone or philosophers' stone. In alchemical lore, this stone was said to turn lead into gold, and it could grant long health, if not immortality, to the alchemist who possessed it.[3] The *Cherubinic Wanderer* includes not only scattered epigrams about this alchemical process but three poetic sequences about it.

The philosophers' stone was known to Angelus in early modern German as the *Stein der Weisen*—literally, the "stone of the wise." The reference to wisdom and the philosophers evoked connections that would not normally occur with the English phrase "sorcerers' stone." For instance, "the stone of the wise" conjures up allusions to the wise men of the Christmas story, who are themselves described as magi or magician-kings from the East, and who offer pure gold to the Christ child. Angelus also refers to the wise man of the biblical Psalms and Proverbs. Such a man, living rightly even in a world full of temptations or distractions, can turn the lead of the human condition into the gold of a virtuous life.

Since the soul can change from lead to gold only with divine help, Angelus often describes God as an alchemist. In God's divine workshop, equipped with tinctures and molds and fires, God puts the human soul through a crucible. The painful experience involves burning, melting, smelting, and smithing, but the end product is a golden image of Himself. In this context, Angelus envisions the "stone of the wise" as divine love, the means by which the soul becomes like God. Angelus also sometimes refers to another stone: the *Ekstein*. By a convenient coincidence, *Ekstein* in Angelus's early modern German can mean both cornerstone (*Eckstein*) and genuine stone (*Echtstein*). A cornerstone is a crucial element in a building, supporting two intersecting walls precisely where stability is most needed. The cornerstone is also a biblical image for Jesus Christ, who is described as the spiritual foundation of those who believe in Him.[4] The further allusion to the "genuine stone" allows Angelus to set up a contrast between Christ as a true stone versus the false

---

3. For recent scholarship on the philosophers' stone and the history of alchemy, see Linden's *Mystical Metal of Gold*. For primary texts in the alchemical tradition, see Linden's *The Alchemy Reader*.

4. See Ephesians 2:19–21.

alchemical stones that do not produce true gold. Some gold is fools' gold, after all, and the alchemical stone that can make physical gold is a poor substitute for the real stone that can make spiritual gold.[5]

The epigrams appearing here thus cover a range of topics. Paramount is the soul's transformation from lead to gold and the contrast between wisdom and foolishness. Above all, the stone of the wise, whether alchemical or spiritual, is not just around for the taking. It must first be looked for. Since the stone of the wise must be sought, the epigrams below teach the reader to look, listen, ask, and journey.

## NOTE ON THE TRANSLATION

The final version of Angelus's *Cherubinic Wanderer* was published in German in 1675 as the *Cherubinischer Wandersmann*. It had 1,676 poems, of which about 100 appear in this translation. Angelus arranged his epigrams in almost no thematic order, apart from a few clusters on related topics. The most profound mystical insights often sit next to witticisms on money or dinner. Despite the jumble, there are consistent themes, and this translation lifts them out so poems on shared topics can be read together.

With the *Cherubinic Wanderer* containing so many epigrams, naturally no full English translation exists. Even the most magisterial (Maria Shrady's) covers only around 800.[6] I've undertaken these new translations for three reasons. First, I focus on themes likely to interest a younger generation, especially readers of fantasy. Though Angelus would not have recognized fantasy as a distinct literary genre in his day, much of his rich imagery meets the criteria for what we would call "the fantastic." With metaphors drawn from medieval alchemy, fantastic beasts, battles, romances, and epics, Angelus uses fictional figures to illuminate the real spiritual life of a Christian.

---

5. For the "Ekstein" as a genuine stone, see epigram 1:280 (p. 19 in this translation). For the "Ekstein" as a cornerstone, see 3:119 (p. 16 below). For either or both meanings at once, see epigrams 1:87 and 3:117 (pp. 18 and 14 below). For a further contrast between real versus false alchemy, see 3:120 (p. 17).

6. See Shrady, *Angelus Silesius*.

Second, my translation differs from previous ones by pulling epigrams liberally from all six books of the *Cherubinic Wanderer* and grouping them thematically. Other translations heavily favor Book 1 or proceed numerically with no emphasis on any particular topic. The result is a very detailed and faithful representation of the first part of Angelus's *Cherubinic Wanderer*, but the beginner will lose the forest for the trees and miss major themes, as well as many entertaining epigrams, from Books 2 through 6.

The third reason for my new translation is that Angelus's epigrams pose peculiar poetic challenges. Angelus combines sharp colloquial witticisms with profound mystical insights, all in the tiny poetic form of a single rhyming couplet. This is hard to render into smooth English poetry. Some previous translators have opted not to translate the epigrams as poetry but as prose. On the other hand, many who do attempt the poetry end up falling back on awkward English constructions to capture both Angelus's sense and his rhymes. Many translations favor archaic English poetic conventions—"thee/thou," inverted word order, obsolete verb forms—all of which make Angelus less lively than his original self.

My translation goes a different way. I use modern colloquial English, while keeping within the constraints of the couplet with its hard end-rhymes. The goal is pithiness and humor rather than awe-inspiring profundity, as Angelus himself clearly intends in many, if not most, of his epigrams.

For readers wanting a closer look at the original, I've included the German text from the 1675 version. This edition is in the public domain.[7] Though I have not always kept the numerical order of the poems, any reader can identify the original placement by using the reference at the end of each poem. The references follow the format "Book: poem number." For instance, "2:13" points to Book 2, epigram 13.

Since readers can look up the original order of the epigrams easily, I have had no hesitation about rearranging the poems when necessary. The goal is to place similar epigrams close enough together to highlight connections that would otherwise be obscured

---

7. For the critical edition, see Gnädinger, *Cherubinischer Wandersmann*.

by distance. Many orders would do, and my present system organizes itself around two main themes. Part 1 presents epigrams with explicit or implicit alchemical content, whether about the philosophers' stone, the alchemists' laboratories, comparisons between gold and the soul, or the natural substances used in alchemy (plants, rocks, fires, the phoenix, etc.). I have grouped these roughly by sub-topics, though many epigrams relate to multiple topics, and the groups blend into each other. Part 2 presents epigrams about the wise man (*der Weise*), who appears not only in the alchemical poems but in many others, pointing to Angelus's broader vision of the life of wisdom versus folly. This section includes epigrams on the wisdom of finding God in nature, the role of time versus eternity, and the value of earthly gold versus true riches. Part 2 concludes with a barrage of poems from Book 6, of which one poem breaks the epigrammatic form and runs to 56 lines, praising the wise man, his activities, and his latter end.

Readers already familiar with Angelus may be interested in some minor changes I've made to the German text. Most notably, I've split each epigram into four lines instead of the original two, both in the German and the translation. This is only a visual aid and does not alter the text or the number of poetic feet. Most of Angelus's poems are two-line hexameters, meaning that there are two lines with six "beats" per line. It is easy to divide two six-foot lines into four three-foot lines, because in either case there is a total of twelve feet, whether counted as six by two or three by four. Only occasionally does the precise line break matter to the text. Very rarely, my translation adds or subtracts a foot for poetic effect, but these are nonstandard cases that the reader can easily track by comparing my English with the German.

The original German punctuation and spelling have been very slightly modified here for readability. I've removed the original slash (/) often used to divide lines, unless it was important to signal unusual breaks in the rhythm or meaning. I've also removed the original double capitals in certain words (GOtt) in favor of single capitals (Gott). However, I've kept the other idiosyncrasies of Angelus's early modern spelling (Jch for ich, Umbkraißfor Umkreis, etc.). The spelling is sometimes important for the sense, since Angelus's early modern usage can create puns or allusions that are more easily lost in twenty-first-century German. To each poem, short as it is, Angelus also gives a title. Since these titles can give as much information as the poem itself, I've translated and included them in bolded letters.

Finally, a note for readers interested in translation method. The translations here are formal but not strictly literal. My reason is that poetry is a marriage of sound and sense, and at times Angelus's poems do not prioritize the sense over the sound. Angelus's charm almost always lies in his snappy or melodic or pithy way of putting things. Thus, some sounds take priority over some senses. When translating, my first step was to decide on Angelus's central point, and the second step was to rank the devices he used to make it. Often both the main point and the devices could be translated well enough in rhyming English. But sometimes Angelus uses literal devices that aren't essential to the poem as such. These non-essentials could be sacrificed.

For instance, Angelus often uses pronouns such as "one" or "someone" or "whoever" (*man, wer*) which can easily convert to "I" or "you," or which can even convert to commands. A good example is the following epigram (5:177):

> Mensch wer dem Herren folgt
> in seinem Thun und lassen,
> der liest deßLebens Buch,
> und kan die Meinung fassen.

A strictly literal translation would be:

> O Man, whoever follows the Lord
> in what He does and allows
> reads the Book of Life
> and grasps its meaning.

A pithier English translation trades in "Man" and "whoever" for a simple command, which gets directly to the point:

> Follow all God's doing,
> both how He wills and does it.
> You'll read the Book of Life

and grasp the meaning of it.

The pithy version more closely echoes Angelus's sound and makes his point despite switching up the pronouns and sentence structure. Conveniently, Angelus's epigrams are so short that the main point is hard to miss. But there are surprisingly many ways to translate a given poem. I am sure ideas for improvements will occur to readers while comparing my English to the German. I hope these translations will spur on more attempts at the game.

Angelus's epigrams range from funny to awe-inspiring, and they are always rewarding. As the first volume in a new series, this book introduces the concept of soul alchemy as one of the many threads in the *Cherubinic Wanderer*. The volumes to follow will each pick up a separate thread: the hero's journey, the soul as an immortal bride, and the divine play that ensues when God creates the world and then redeems it in a cosmic drama.

Rachel Lott
Toronto, Ontario

# PART 1

## The Sorcerers' Stone

## WHAT IS GOOD IS WHAT ENDURES

Pure as finest gold,
stern as solid granite,
crystal-clear, and clearer:
this shall be your spirit.


## WAS FEIN IST DAS BESTEHT

Rein wie das feinste Gold
steiff wie ein Felsenstein
gantz lauter wie Cristall
sol dein Gemüthe seyn.

(1:1)

## SPIRITUAL GOLD-MAKING

Lead becomes essential gold
of purest quality,
when in my God and through my God,
I turn to deity.

## DIE GEISTLICHE GOLDMACHUNG

Dann wird das Bley zu Gold,
dann fällt der Zufall hin,
wann ich mit Gott durch Gott
in Gott verwandelt bin.

(1:102)[1]

---

1. This is the beginning of the first sequence on spiritual alchemy in the *Cherubinic Wanderer*. The sequence includes epigrams 1:102–4, reproduced here in order, and is followed by a second, longer sequence of epigrams in 1:244–50.

## ON THE SAME TOPIC

I am myself the metal.
The Spirit fires my soul.
Messiah is the tincture
that purifies the whole.

## AUCH VON DERSELBEN

Jch selbst bin das Metall,
der Geist ist Feur und Herd,
Messias die Tinctur,
die Leib und Seel verklärt.

(1:103)

## STILL ON THE SAME TOPIC

God puts me through the fire.
He melts me, smiths, and smelts,
until I'm soft enough,
then stamps me with Himself.

## NOCH VON JHR

So bald durch Gottes Feur
ich mag geschmeltzet seyn,
So drukt mir Gott alßbald
sein eigen Wesen ein.

(1:104)

## LOVE IS THE SORCERERS' STONE

The sorcerers' stone is love.
It makes gold out of ash,
turns nothings into things,
and makes us God at last.[2]

## DIE LIEBE IST DER WEISEN STEIN

Lieb' ist der weisen Stein:
sie scheidet Gold außkoth,
sie machet nichts zu jchts,
und wandelt mich in Gott.

(1:244)

2. Thus begins the second and longer sequence on spiritual alchemy in the *Cherubinic Wanderer*. The sequence includes epigrams 1:244–50, translated here in order.

## THERE MUST BE UNION

You want a transmutation
away from pain or worse?
Then love must join your nature
to God's own nature first.

## ES MUß VEREINIGT WERDEN

Jm fall die Liebe dich
versetzen sol auß Peyn,
Muß deine Menschheit vor
mit Gottes Eines seyn.

(1:245)

## THE TINCTURE

The Holy Ghost extracts the ore.
The Father tests and tries it.
The tincture turning all to gold?—
the Son. He purifies it.

## DIE TINGIERUNG

Der heilge Geist der schmeltzt,
der Vater der verzehrt,
der Sohn ist die Tinctur,
die Gold macht und verklärt.

(1:246)

## THE OLD HAS PASSED AWAY

You can't say gold is iron.
As little as you can,
you'll see humanity
and know it in the man.

## DAS ALTE IST HINWEG

So wenig du das Gold
kanst schwartz und Eisen nennen:
so wenig wirstu dort
den Mensch am Menschen kennen.

(1:247)

## THE REAL UNION

See the lead receive the gold-hood—
how united they become!
Thus the essence of the Godhead
joins the Godded[3] into one.

## DIE GENAUE VEREINIGUNG

Schau doch wie hoch Vereint
die Goldheit mit dem Bley,
und der Vergöttete
mit Gottes wesen sey!

(1:248)

3. A rare but literal translation of *Vergöttete*—someone who has been made God. For a similar use in contemporary English, see C. S. Lewis: "She is so lately godded that she is still a rather poor goddess." (*Till We Have Faces*, chapter 21, p. 241).

## GOLDHOOD AND GODHOOD

What makes you gold is gold-hood.
What makes you God is God-hood.
What are you, then, without them?
A lump of lead and mud-hood.

## DIE GOLDHEIT UND GOTTHEIT

Die Goldheit machet Gold,
die Gottheit machet Gott:
Wirstu nicht eins mit ihr,
so bleibstu Bley und Koth.

(1:249)

## AS GOLDHOOD, SO GODHOOD

See the weight of glory
the gold-hood gives the gold.
This is, among the holy,
what Godhead gives the soul.

## WIE DIE GOLDHEIT ALSO DIE GOTTHEIT

Schau wie die Goldheit ist
deß Golds fluß, schwer' und schein:
so wird die Gottheit auch
im seelgen alles seyn.

(1:250)

## THE CORNERSTONE IS BEST

The stone for making gold
is much sought after.
Why not the Cornerstone,
for wealth and health hereafter?

## DER EKSTEIN IST DAS BESTE

Den Goldstein suchet man,
und läst den Ekkestein,
Durch den man ewig reich,
gesund, und klug kan seyn!

(3:117)[4]

4. This is the beginning of the most explicit sequence on the sorcerers' stone in the *Cherubinic Wanderer*. It includes epigrams 3:117–20, which are translated here in order. In these epigrams, Angelus contrasts the sorcerers' stone of alchemy with the "cornerstone" that makes real spiritual gold. For a discussion of the contrast, see the Introduction, pp. ix–x.

## THE SORCERERS' STONE IS WITHIN

Friend, go within yourself.
The fabled sorcerers' stone
is not a thing to seek
in foreign lands alone.

## DER WEISEN STEIN IST IN DIR

Mensch geh nur in dich selbst.
Denn nach dem Stein der weisen
Darf man nicht allererst
in frembde Lande reisen.

(3:118)

## THE CORNERSTONE MAKES WHAT LASTS

The stone for making gold
will make what wears away.
The Cornerstone will make
a home to stay.


## DER EKSTEIN MACHT WAS EWIG WEHRT

Der Goldstein machet Gold
das mit der Welt vergeht:
der Ekstein einen Bau
der ewiglich besteht.

(3:119)

## THE BEST POTION

He is a potion-master
for real, and not a fraud,
who turns his heart to gold
for very love of God.

## DIE BESTE TINGIRUNG

Den halt ich im Tingirn
für Meister und bewehrt
der Gott zu Lieb sein Hertz
ins feinste Gold verkehrt.

(3:120)

## WITH THE CORNERSTONE IS TREASURE

Why plague the poor physician?
Your help is here alone.
Health, wealth, and every art
come from the Cornerstone.


## JM EKSTEIN LIEGT DER SCHATZ

Was marterstu das ärtzt:
der Ekstein ists allein
jn dem Gesundheit, Gold,
und alle Künste seyn.

(1:87)

## THE TRUE SORCERERS' STONE

The chemist's stone is nothing.
The real stone,[5] in my eyes,
is here: my golden tincture,
the Stone of all the Wise.

## DER WAHRE WEISEN STEIN

Dein stein Chymist ist nichts:
der Ekstein den ich mein
jst meine Gold Tinctur,
und aller weisen Stein.

(1:280)

5. Though *Ekstein* usually means cornerstone, here Angelus intends *Echtstein* (genuine stone). The epigram opposes the real stone of the wise to the false stone of the alchemist.

## THE WORKING OF THE
## HOLY SACRAMENTS

The bread of God in us
works like the sorcerers' stone.
It smelts and purifies
until we're gold alone.[6]

## DIE WÜRCKUNG DEß
## HEILIGEN SACRAMENTS

Das Brodt der Herr in uns
wirkt wie der weisen stein:
Es machet uns zu Gold,
wo wir geschmoltzen seyn.

(5:119)

6. The "bread of God" refers to the bread eaten during the Catholic cel-
ebration of the Eucharist. Smelting is a process of heating a metal to extract
impurities. Angelus thus portrays the Eucharistic bread as an efficient means
by which God transforms the soul and purifies it of corruption.

## THE SPIRITUAL ARK AND ITS MANNA

Man, if your heart is gold,
and if your soul is clean,
you are the Ark of God
and angels' bread within.[7]

## DIE GEISTLICHE ARCH UND'S MANNA-KRÜGLEIN

Mensch ist dein Hertze Gold
und deine Seele rein
so kanst auch du die Arch
und's Mannakrüglein seyn.

(1:196)

7. Though this epigram and the next do not mention the sorcerers' stone explicitly, they expand on the Eucharistic reference of epigram 5:119. The "angels' bread" is the manna in the book of Exodus, where God provides bread from heaven for the Israelites in the wilderness. When Moses constructs the ark of the covenant, he places manna inside as a memorial. In Christian literature, the manna in the ark is often identified as an archetype of Christ's body in the tomb or in the Eucharist. Angelus's next epigram (1:197), translated on the following page, affirms God's gradual work of bringing the soul to perfection. The juxtaposition of the two epigrams indicates that Angelus sees a strong link between the Eucharistic bread and God's transformative work in the soul.

## GOD BRINGS TO PERFECTION

I, too, shall have perfection,
as God has willed long since.
Deny this, and you disbelieve
omnipotence.


## GOTT MACHT VOLLKOMMEN SEYN

Daß Gott Allmächtig sey
das glaubet jener nicht
der mir Vollkommenheit /
wie Gott begehrt / abspricht.

(1:197)

## THE TINCTURE

Look at the chemist's tincture.
You'll see how fair and free
your own salvation is,
the change to deity.


## DAS TINGIREN

Betrachte das Tingirn
so sihstu schön und frey
Wie dein' Erlösung
und wie die Vergöttung sey.

(1:258)

## ACCIDENT AND ESSENCE

O man: become essential!
When the world is gone,
the accidents will fail.
The essence carries on.[8]

## ZUFALL UND WESEN

Mensch werde wesentlich:
denn wann die Welt vergeht
so fällt der Zufall weg /
das wesen das besteht.

(2:30)

8. Aristotelian philosophy distinguishes between a thing's essence and its "accidents." Accidents are qualities that a thing happens to have but can lose without affecting the essence. In Angelus's day, the essence of a human being was expressed with the formula "man is a rational animal." Accidents like social position or wealth could change without affecting that essence. Here Angelus raises the question of what will remain when the accidents of human life vanish entirely.

## IT MUST BE TURNED TO GOLD

Take gold and overlay
the many works you do,
or else God won't be pleased
with either them or you.

## ES MUß VERGOLDET SEYN

Christ alles was du thust
das überzeuch mit Gold:
Sonst ist Gott weder dir
noch deinen Werken hold.

(2:130)

## THE GOLD-MAKING OF THE WISE

The wise can alter nature.
They make gold by their art—
and most when virtue makes us
angel-like at heart.

## DEß WEISEN GOLDMACHUNG

Der Weise machet Gold,
verändert Ertz und Stein,
wann er die Tugend pflantzt,
und unß macht Englisch seyn.

(3:208)

## THE FACE OF GOD MAKES BLESSED

The face of God attracts
like iron magnetized.[9]
A glimpse is all you need
to be beatified.

## DAS ANTLITZ GOTTES IST SEELIGMACHEND

Das Antlitz Gottes zeucht
an sich wie Eisenstein:
Nur einen Blik es schaun
macht ewig seelig seyn.

(5:272)

---

9. A rare use of magnetism as a metaphor for God. Though Angelus does not use the word for magnet, he describes God as the *Eisenstein* (iron stone) which *zeucht an sich* (attracts to itself).

## THE EAGLE FLIES HIGH

How high the eagle soars!
Whoever is like him
can reach the thousandth heaven
beyond the seraphim.[10]

## DER ADLER FLEUGET HOCH

Ja wer ein Adler ist
der kan sich wol erschwingen
und über Seraphim
durch tausend Himmel dringen.

(2:171)

10. This is the first in a sequence of four epigrams using birds as metaphors for the soul. The sequence starts with the eagle and includes the phoenix, an unspecified "little bird," and the dove. Alchemical texts used such birds as symbols for elements or processes. Probably Angelus intends this use for the phoenix, and possibly for the eagle, though his use of the other two birds is not so clear. The epigrams are translated in order below. For instances of birds used symbolically in alchemy, see Linden, *The Alchemy Reader*, 116, 133, 147, and 246.

## BECOME A PHOENIX

I wish I were a phoenix.
I'd burn with such desire
that none could sift my ash
from God's all-burning fire.

## EIN PHOENIX SOL MAN SEYN

Jch wil ein Phoenix seyn,
und mich in Gott verbrennen
damit mich nur nichts mehr
von Jhme könne trennen.

(2:172)

## THE WEAK MUST WAIT

Not yet, poor little bird.
You can't fly on your own.
So wait here patiently,
until your wings have grown.


## DIE SCHWACHEN MÜSSEN WARTEN

Du armes Vögelein,
kanstu nicht selber fliegen,
so bleibe mit Geduld
biß du mehr krafft hast ligen.

(2:173)

## YOU MUST TRY

Try, my little dove.
You'll learn from every drill.
The way to reach the goal
is by not sitting still.

## ES WIL GEÜBET SEYN

Versuch mein Däubelein:
mit übung lernt man viel:
Wer nur nicht sitzen bleibt,
der kombt doch noch zum Ziel.

(2:174)

## TO EACH ITS OWN ELEMENT

The fish all live in water.
The birds? within the air.
The plants? the solid earth.
The sun? the firmament.
The flaming salamander?
The fiery flame is where.
And I?
In Jesu's heart,
my proper element.[11]

11. In pre-modern times, physical things were thought to consist of the four elements of earth, air, fire, and water. A fifth element was sometimes said to compose the things beyond the moon, such as the stars and planets. Not only did the elements constitute things, they also served as habitats for them. Here Angelus identifies the five major habitats and the things that inhabit them. Earth is the domain of plants, water of aquatic animals, air of flying animals, and the firmament of the sun. Angelus even repeats the widespread belief that fire was a habitat for salamanders. But his main point is the last. What element serves as the proper habitat for the human soul? Only the heart of Jesus.

## EINS JEDEN ELEMENT

Jm Wasser lebt der Fisch
die Pflantzen in der Erden
der Vogel in der Lufft
die Sonn im Firmament:
der Salamander muß
im Feur erhalten werden:
Jm Hertzen JESU ich
als meinem Element.

(4:32)

## THE TRANSFIGURATION

When once the flame has burnt
what made it gross and dull,
my body too will shine
like God's own carbuncle.[12]

## DIE VERKLÄRUNG

Mein Leib der wird für Gott
wie ein Carfunkel stehn
wenn seine grobheit wird
im Feuer untergehn.

(2:110)

---

12. The remaining epigrams in this section involve fire, melting, or other forms of purification.

In medieval gemology, carbuncles were thought to have special light-giving properties. The Latin word *carbunculus* means a small piece of coal or charcoal. Coal is dark and cold on its own, but fiery red when lit. For more on carbuncle symbolism, see Dell'Acqua, "The Carbunculus," 158–72.

## THE SOUL COMES FROM GOD

From God, the lightning bolt,
the soul has shot forth burning.
No wonder it should seek
a swift returning!

## DIE SEELE KOMBT VON GOTT

Die Seel ist eine Flamm
auß Gott dem Blitz gegangen:
ach solte sie dann nicht
in Jhn zurük gelangen.

(2:158)

## GOD WORKS LIKE FIRE

The flame melts all to one.
Return to God again,
and in that ancient source
be molten into Him.


## GOTT WÜRKET WIE DAS FEWR

Das Fewer schmeltzt und eint:
sinckstu inn Ursprung ein
so muß dein Geist mit Gott
in Eins geschmeltzet seyn.

(2:163)

## THERE MUST BE SEPARATION

Guiltlessness is gold.
No dirt is mixed with it.
You wish to be like that?
Scrub off the grime and grit.

## DIE SCHEIDUNG MUß GESCHEHN

Die Unschuld ist ein Gold
das keine Schlakken hat:
entzeuch dich auß dem Kiß
so bistu's in der that.

(2:170)

## YOU CAN DEAL WITH THE ENEMY

Burn, my child, in God,
and be a living flame.
You'll be the devil's darkness
and Belial's bane.

## DU KANST DEM FEIND VERGEBEN

Entbrenne doch mein Kind
und sey ein Licht in Gott:
So bistu Belials Gifft
Finsternüß und Tod.

(2:247)

## MAN IS COAL

You're just a lump of coal.
God is the fire and light.
If you don't live in Him,
you're dark and cold as night.

## DER MENSCH IST EINE KOHLE

Mensch, du bist eine Kohl:
Gott ist dein Feur und Licht:
du bist schwartz, finster, kalt,
liegstu in Jhme nicht.

(4:133)

## HOW LOVE CONSUMES SINS

Look how the flax and fluff
consume within the fire.
So may your sins consume
in love's desire.


## WIE DIE LIEB DIE SÜNDEN VERZEHRT

Wie du den Flachs unds Werk
im Feuer sichst verschwinden.
So brennen auch hinweg
durch Liebe deine Sünden.

(4:152)

## THE SPIRITUAL LIGHTER

The tinder is my will,
the lighter is my heart;
the whole will catch on fire,
if God just strikes a spark.


## DER GEISTLICHE FEUERZEUG

Mein Hertz ists Feuerzeug,
der Zunder gutter Wille:
Schlaegt Gott ein Fuenklein drein,
so brennts und leuchts die voelle.

(5:47)

## AS YOU ARE, SO YOU ARE AFFECTED

The sun—the selfsame sun—
melts wax and hardens coal.
That's how, to life or death,
God works upon your soul.


## WIE DU BIST, SO WIRSTU GEWUERKET

Die Sonn erweicht das Wachss
und machet hart den Koth:
So wirkt auch Gott nach dir
das Leben und den Tod.

(5:58)

## THE CROSS IS THE TEST OF LOVE

The fire tries the gold
for purity or dross.
The purity of love
is tested by the Cross.

## DAS KREUTZ PROBIRT DIE LIEBE

Jm Feuer wird das Gold
obs reine sey probirt,
und deine Lieb im Kreutz,
wie lauter sie, gespürt.

(5:304)

## A RICH SINNER IS A GOLD-COVERED PIECE OF COAL

Though you cover it with gilding,
a coal is still a coal.
Though a sinner stands in gold,
he has a sinner's soul.

## EIN REICHER SÜNDER EIN VERGOLDTER KOTH

Mensch kein vergoldter Koth
ist reich geehrt und schön:
die Sünder auch / die gleich
in lautrem Golde stehn.

(6:28)

## THE FIRE IN GOD'S SMITHY

Jealousy is fire.
For others' good once lit,
God forges thunderbolts
of love from it.

## GOTTES SCHMIEDE FEUER

Der Eifer ist ein Feur:
brent er umbs Nächsten Heil,
so schmiedet Gott darbey
der Liebe Donnerkeil.

(6:228)

## HOW TO BECOME WISE

To know yourself and God,
and to be wise, O Man,
take all your worldly lust
and burn up all you can.


## WIE MAN WEISE WIRD

Mensch wiltu Weise seyn
wilt Gott und dich erkennen
so mustu vor in dir
die Welt begihr verbrennen.

(6:258)

# PART 2

## The Wise Man

# THE HOUSE OF ETERNAL WISDOM

Eternal Wisdom builds,
and with her I become
the palace where she rests
when she is done.[13]

# DER EWIGEN WEIßHEIT HAUß

Die Ewge Weißheit baut:
jch werde der Pallast:
wann sie in mir / und ich
in jhr gefunden rast.

(1:186)

---

13. In this epigram Angelus envisions wisdom as a goal while the soul is a
work in progress. However, most of his poems about wisdom describe the end
product, the man who has already become wise. In arranging these poems, I
have adopted the following order. First are epigrams with general descriptions
of the wise man or the fool. Second are epigrams about the wise man's specific
attributes. Angelus highlights the wise man's ability to see God in the world, to
rightly use books and other forms of learning, to look into eternity, and to lay
up riches in heaven. Third and finally, I include an unusually long poem from
Book 6. The poem presents the totality of Angelus's vision of the wise man in
the *Cherubinic Wanderer*.

## THE WISDOM OF SOLOMON

Was Solomon the wisest man?
You think it's true?
But you can be both Solomon
and Wisdom too.

## DIE WEIßHEIT SALOMONS

Wie? schätzstu Salomon
den weisesten Allein?
Du auch kanst Salomon
und seine Weißheit seyn.

(2:18)

## A FOOL SEEKS MANY THINGS

The wise seek just one thing,
and that the highest good.
The fool seeks many things,
and nothing as he should.

## EIN NARR SUCHT VIELERLEI

Der weise sucht nur eins,
und zwar das höchste Gut:
ein Narr nach vielerley,
und kleinem streben thut.

(3:171)

## WISDOM IS A WELLSPRING

Wisdom is a wellspring.
The more you drink from her,
she bubbles up and flows
the more and merrier.

## DIE WEIßHEIT IST EIN QUAL

Die Weißheit ist ein Qual:
je mehr man auß jhr trinkt,
je mehr und mächtiger
sie wieder treibt und springt.

(3:213)

## THE THREE SPIRITUAL WISE MEN

The Wise Men bring three gifts.
They bring them, Lord, through me.
The flesh brings weeping myrrh;
the soul, her golden love;
the spirit offers prayer
like frankincense above.
O let me ever be
wise as these wisest Three!


## DIE DREY GEISTLICHE WEISEN

Drey Weisen tragen Gott
in mir drey Gaben an:
Der Leib zerknirschungs Myrrhn,
die Seele Gold der Liebe,
der Geist den Weyherauch
der Andacht wie er kan:
Ach daß ich jmmerdar
so dreymal Weise bliebe!


(3:240)

## THE FIRM ROCK

A man of virtue is
a rock upon firm ground.
Let storms come as they will:
he won't fall down.[14]

## DER STEIFFE FELSENSTEIN

Ein tugendthaffter Mensch
ist wie ein Felsenstein:
Es stürme wie es wil
er fället doch nicht ein.

(5:20)

14. This epigram alludes to the parable of the wise man and the fool in Matthew 7:24–27. The wise man builds his house on a rock, while the fool builds on sand. When a storm comes, it destroys the fool's house but not the wise man's. Notably, Angelus highlights virtue and not knowledge as the crucial difference. The passage in Matthew describes the wise man hearing the words of Christ *and acting on them*. The fool hears but does not act.

## NEGLIGENCE DOES NOT REACH GOD

You say you'll gladly see
God and His light one day?
O fool: that's what you'll never see
if not today.

## NACHLÄSSIGKEIT KOMT NICHT ZU GOTT

Du sprichst du wirst noch wohl
Gott sehen und sein Licht:
O Narr du siehst ihn nie
siehstu ihn heute nicht.

(6:115)

## THE FOOL CHOOSES THE WORST

You'd rather have the world
than heaven in its beauty?
A fool prefers the sticks
before the king's own city.


## DER NARR ERKIEST DAS ÄRGSTE

Ein Narr ist / der den Stok
fürs Kaisers Burg erkiest;
der lieber in der Welt
als in dem Himmel ist.

(6:123)

## THE WISE MAN SEEKS NOTHING

A wise man seeks for nothing.
He has the stillest order.
And why? In God he turns
to something wholly other.

## DER WEISE SUCHT NICHTS

Der weise suchet nichts,
er hat den stillsten Orden:
warumb? er ist in Gott
schon alles selber worden.

(6:183)

## THE WORK OF THE WISE AND FOOLISH

This is the wise man's work:
becoming God at last.
The fool takes many pains
becoming dust and ash.


## DES WEISEN UND NARREN WERK

Des Weisen gantzes Werk
ist daß er werde Gott:
Der Narr bemühet sich
biß er wird Erd und Koth.

(6:230)

## THE SINNER TURNS TO ASHES

The holy ones climb up
and turn to God above.
The sinners tumble down
and turn to ash and mud.[15]

## DER SÜNDER WIRD ZU KOTH

Der Heilge steiget auf
und wird ein Gott in Gott:
der Sünder fällt herab
und wird zu Mist und Koth.

(6:29)

15. Angelus often echoes this contrast between the wise man or the saint on one hand, and the fool or sinner on the other. Wisdom and holiness together lead the soul toward divinity, while folly and sin lead to ultimate corruption.

## THE WISE MAN IS NEVER ALONE

The wise man's not alone.
He walks apart from you,
and yet the Lord of all
is walking with him too.

## DER WEISE IST NIE ALLEIN

Der Weiß ist nie allein,
geht er gleich ohne dich:
so hat er doch den Herrn
der dinge (Gott) mit sich.

(6:242)

## THE ECCENTRIC

A fool would build on sand.
But on the thoughts of men
you build your house instead.
Are you much wiser, then?[16]

## AN DEN SONDERLING

Die Meinungen seind Sand,
ein Narr der bauet drein.
Du baust auf Meinungen:
wie kanstu weise sein?

(6:251)

16. Another allusion to Matthew 7:24–27. Cf. p. 54 above.

## TRUTH MAKES ONE WISE

The truth is just what is.
Where it's not recognized,
the one who cannot see
cannot be reckoned wise.

## DIE WARHEIT MACHT WEISE SEYN

Die Wahrheit giebt das seyn:
wer sie nicht recht erkennt
Der wird mit keinem recht
ein Weiser Mann genennt.

(6:261)

## GOD GIVES THE GREAT IN THE SMALL

Take what God has given.
The great is in the small;
the gold is in the dross,
though we neglect it all.[17]

## GOTT GIEBT DAS GROß' IM KLEINEN

Nimb was der Herr dir giebt:
Er giebt das groß im kleinen,
in schlechten schlakken Gold,
ob wirs zwar nicht vermeinen.

(4:14)

17. Several poems in Book 4 are about the wise man's ability to find the great in the small. The epigrams translated on this topic include 4:158–62 below.

## THE GREAT IS HIDDEN IN THE SMALL

The circle's in the point,
the fruit is in the seed:
seek God within the world,
and you are wise indeed.[18]

## DAS GROSSE IST IM
## KLEINEN VERBORGEN

Der Umbkraiß ist im Punckt,
im Saamen liegt die Frucht,
Gott in der Welt: wie Klug
ist der jhn drinne sucht!

(4:158)

18. This epigram introduces a sequence about the wisdom of looking for
God in the world (epigrams 4:158–62). The language echoes alchemical lan-
guage about finding the macrocosm in the microcosm. Angelus's point is not
that God is part of the material world, or that the material world is part of
God. Indeed, many of Angelus's epigrams underscore the radical otherness
of God. See for instance epigram 6:262 on p. 71 below, which sets up a direct
contradiction to the sequence here. Angelus's point here is that the world is a
limited means of learning about God. For the relationship of macrocosm to
microcosm in alchemy, see Linden, *The Alchemy Reader*, 15–16; and Schuler,
*Alchemical Poetry*, 53.

## EVERYTHING IS IN EVERYTHING

All things are in all things.
Saint Benedict, of course,
looked on a beam of light
and saw the universe.

## ALLES IST ALLEM

Wie sah S. Benedict
die Welt in einem strahl?
Es ist (weistu's noch nicht?)
in allem alls zumahl.

(4:159)

## GOD IS EVERYWHERE SPLENDOROUS

No speck of dust or dirt,
no single mote so small,
but that the wise man sees
God's glory in it all.


## GOTT IST ÜBERALL HERRLICH

Kein Stäublein ist so schlecht,
kein Stöpffchin ist so klein:
Der Weise sihet Gott
gantz Herrlich drinne seyn.

(4:160)

## ALL IN ONE

They're in a mustard seed,
if you will only see them:
an image of all things
in hell and earth and heaven.

## ALLES IN EINEM

Jn einem Senffkörnlein
so du's verstehen wilt
ist aller oberern
und untrern dinge Bild.

(4:161)

## ONE IS IN ANOTHER

The hen is in the egg,
the egg is in the hen:
two things are in the one,
and one in two things then.

## EINS IST IM ANDREN

Das Ey ist in der Henn,
die Henn ist in dem Ey:
Die zwey im Eins, und auch
das Eines in der Zwey.

(4:162)

## AS CREATURES IN GOD

A tree within a seed,
a fire in a spark:
if you would look on God,
look on His handiwork.


## WIE DIE CREATUR IN GOTT

Wie du das Feur im Kieß
den Baum im Kern sichst seyn:
So bild dir das Geschöpff
in Gott dem Schöpffer ein.

(4:185)

# THE TRINITY IN NATURE

A single plant can show you
that God's a Trinity.
Behold the three in one:
salt, sulfur, mercury.[19]

# DIE DREYEINIGKEIT IN DER NATUR

Daß Gott Dreyeinig ist
zeigt dir ein jedes Kraut
da Schwefel / Saltz / Mercur
in einem wird geschaut.

(1:257)

19. This epigram alludes to Paracelsus's alchemical theory that natural objects in the world are formed by the three elements of salt, sulfur, and mercury. For more on Paracelsus, see Linden, *The Alchemy Reader*, 151–69. In Angelus's reasoning, if three elements can combine to make up a single object like a plant, then there can hardly be a problem with three persons making up a single God.

# THE WORLD IS A GRAIN

Why can't we see our God
within the world at hand?
It strains the eye too much:
the world's a grain of sand.[20]


# DIE WELT IST EIN SANDKORN

Wie daß denn bey der Welt
Gott nicht geschaut kan seyn?
Sie kränkt das Auge stets:
sie ist ein Sandkörnlein.

(6:262)

20. Angelus loves paradox. He sometimes contradicts his own epigrams in
order to underscore a different point. On the relationship of this epigram to
the sequence above about seeking God in the world, see note 18 above.

## NOTHING IS GREAT ON EARTH

To heaven, all the world
is just a speck of dirt.
How foolish, then, to think
there's something great on earth!

## NICHTS IST GROß AUF DER ERDE

Zum Himmel ist die Erd'
ein eintzigs Stäubelein:
O Narr wie kan in ihr
dann etwas grosses seyn?

(6:218)

## THE BOOK OF LIFE

God is the Book of Life.
I'm written with a pen
dipped in the Lamb's own blood.
Shall He not love me, then?[21]

## DAS LEBENS BUCH

Gott ist deß Lebens Buch
ich steh in ihm geschrieben
mit seines Lammes Blutt:
wie solt er mich nicht lieben?

(2:20)

---

21. In Books 2–5, a number of epigrams involve books, schools, or other media of learning. They are translated in order here.

## THE BOOK OF KNOWLEDGE

What's written on my soul
from the beginning?
Fear God and love Him more
than any being.

## DAS BUCH DEß GEWISSENS

Daß ich Gott fürchten sol
und über alles lieben
jst mir von Anbegin
in mein Gemütt geschrieben.

(2:36)

## THE LETTER WITHOUT THE
## SPIRIT IS NOTHING

The letter's just the letter.
I want the verity,
where God may speak His Word
eternally in me.

## SCHRIFFT OHNE GEIST IST NICHTS

Die Schrifft ist Schrifft sonst nichts.
Mein Trost ist Wesenheit
Und daß Gott in mir spricht
das Wort der Ewigkeit.

(2:137)

## HOLY WRIT

A spider can suck out
a poison from the rose.
That's how God's holy word
is treated by its foes!

## DIE HEILIGE SCHRIFFT

Gleich wie die Spinne saugt
auss einer Rose Gifft:
also wird auch verkehrt
vom boesen Gottesschrift!

(4:82)

## THE MAKER IN THE MADE

Creation is a book,
and they who wisely read it
will find within its pages
the very one who made it.

## DER SCHÖPFFER IM GESCHÖPFFE

Die Schöpffung ist ein Buch;
Wer's weißlich lesen kan
dem wird darinn gar fein
der Schöpffer kundt gethan.

(5:86)

## ONE BOOK IS BEST

Much study is much sorrow.
To be forever wise,
a single book is needful—
I mean my Jesus Christ.

## EINS IST DAS BESTE BUCH

Viel Bücher viel beschwehr:
Wer eines recht gelesen
(jch meine Jesum Christ)
ist ewiglich genesen.

(5:87)

## LIFE MUST BE WRITTEN
## IN YOU YOURSELF

If your heart is not
the Book of Life, in essence,
you'll never be read out
into God's presence.

## DAS LEBEN MUSS DIR SELBST
## EINGESCHRIEBEN SEYN

Mensch wird dein Hertze nicht
das Buch deß Lebens seyn:
so wirstu nimmermehr
zu Gott gelassen ein.

(5:106)

## THE ONE WHO READS THE BOOK OF LIFE

Follow all God's doing,
both how He wills and does it.
You'll read the Book of Life
and grasp the meaning of it.


## WER DAS BUCH DEß LEBENS LIESET

Mensch wer dem Herren folgt
in seinem Thun und lassen,
Der liest deß Lebens Buch,
und kan die Meinung fassen.

(5:177)

## LIKE SCHOOL, LIKE STUDENT

Our schools can tell of God
a little at the most.
What school will help us love Him?
That of the Holy Ghost.

## WIE DIE SCHULE SO DIE LEHRE

Jnn Schulen dieser Welt
wird Gott unß nur beschrieben:
Jns Heilgen Geistes Schul
lernt man Jhn schaun und lieben.

(5:267)

## WHERE TO LEARN DIVINE COURTLINESS

My child, to be a courtier
where God is ruling,
go to the Holy Spirit first
and get some schooling.

## WO MAN DIE GÖTTLICHE
## HÖFFLIGKEIT LERNT

Kind wer in Gottes Hof
gedänket zubestehn,
der muß zum Heilgen Geist
hier in die Schule gehn.

(5:342)

## WISDOM WITHOUT LOVE IS NOTHING

If you are wise and don't love God,
then as a rule,
I say it's better far
to be a fool.

## WEIßHEIT OHNE LIEBE IST NICHTS

Mensch wo du weise bist
und liebst nicht Gott darbey:
So sag ich daß ein Narr
dir vorzuziehen sey.

(5:294)

## WHAT THE WISE ACCOMPLISH

A fool is very busy.
The wise? He gives his days
to something tenfold nobler:
to love, and rest, and gaze.

## DEß WEISEN VERRICHTUNG

Ein Narr ist viel bemüht:
deß Weisen gantzes thun
das zehnmal Edeler
ist Lieben / schauen / ruhn.

(5:363)

## THE SOUL'S EYES

Your soul, it has two eyes.
One sees what Time can see,
the other looks away
into Eternity.[22]

## DIE AUGEN DER SEELE

Zwey Augen hat die Seel:
eins schauet in die Zeit,
das andre richtet sich
hin in die Ewigkeit.

(3:228)

22. Angelus often contrasts time and eternity. In many cases Angelus's point is mystical, relating to the timelessness of God. But sometimes he also highlights the wise man's interaction with time. The handful of following epigrams represent the latter emphasis.

## ETERNITY IS NOT MEASURED

Eternity knows nothing
of years or days or hours.
Alas! I have not found
that center point of hers.

## DIE EWIGKEIT WIRD NICHT GEMESSEN

Die Ewigkeit weiß nichts
von Jahren, Tagen, Stunden.
Ach daß ich doch noch nicht
den Mittelpunct gefunden!

(2:65)

## TO THE SINNER

O sinner, just consider
the time you're briefly in,
and then Eternity—
and you will cease to sin.


## AN DEN SÜNDER

O Sünder wann du wol
bedächst das kurtze Nun
und dann die Ewigkeit
du würdst nichts böses thun.

(3:55)

## THE GREATEST FOOL

For worldly things, you'll cast
eternal things away.
Is there in all the world
a greater fool? Do say.


## DER GRÖSTE NARR

Du schlägst umbs Zeitliche
das Ewig' in den wind:
Richt' / ob die Welt auch 'wol
einn grössern Narren findt?

(6:19)

## IT'S FOOLISH TO DO
## ANYTHING BUT BELIEVE

Aren't all you Christians fools?
"Eternity!" you say,
and cling with soul and body
to the present day.

## ANDERST THUN ALS GLAUBEN
## IST NÄRRISCH

Christ bistu nicht ein Narr?
du glaubst die Ewigkeit
und hängst mit Leib und Seel
verblendet an der Zeit!

(6:212)

## THERE MUST BE A PROFIT

O servant, turn a profit
on all your little hoard.
The Profiteer approves.
Who is he, then?
The Lord.[23]

## ES MUSS GEWUCHERT SEYN

Knecht, wuchre dass du hast:
den wann der Herr wird kommen:
So wird von ihm allein
der Wuchrer angenommen.

(2:222)

23. Many of Angelus's epigrams comment on the wise man's attitude toward earthly riches. The poems translated through the rest of this section contrast the wise man with the miser. The wise man knows the proper place for gold, but the miser hoards it at the cost of his soul.

The epigram above alludes to the parable of the wise and foolish servants in Matthew 25:14–30. As the story relates, a rich man known for his skill in profiteering goes on a journey. Before leaving, he divides his money into three shares and entrusts them to three servants. Two of those servants invest their shares wisely and present their master with capital gains when he returns. The third servant buries his share and returns it as it is. The master threatens this foolish servant with apocalyptic punishment, since he could at least have put the money in the bank to earn interest. Angelus's point (and the parable's as well) is not about the virtue of profiteering but about the wise use of whatever we have, with an eye to eternity.

## THE HOLY KINGDOM

Be poor. The holy ones
have nothing left
but what they do not want:
the flesh of death.

## DEß HEILIGEN REICHTHUMB

Sey arm: der Heylige
hat nichts in dieser Zeit
als was er ungern hat,
den Leib der Sterblichkeit.

(3:69)

## TO THE SINNER

The richest of the demons
owns not a single pebble.
How poor your lot must be!
You serve the poorest devil.

## AN DEN SUENDER

Der reichste Teuffel hat
nicht einen Kieselstein:
Du bist des aermbsten Sclav:
kan auch was aermers seyn?

(3:96)

## WHAT YOU SEEK IS WHAT YOU FIND

The rich men seek for gold;
the poor seek God Himself.
The poor will have the gold,
the rich will have the pelf.

## WAS MAN SUCHT DAS FINDT MAN

Der Reiche suchet Gold,
der arme suchet Gott:
Gold find der arme Mensch
warhafftig, jener Koth.

(3:139)

## SOMETIMES GREED IS GOOD

The greedy fight and grapple
for things that pass away.
Why don't we do the same
for what will stay!


## DER GEITZ IST MANCHMAL GUT

Der Geitzhalß scharrt und kratzt
umb zeitlichen Gewin:
Ach daß wir unß nicht so
umb ewigen bemühn!

(3:167)

## THE CROSS

The Cross is what I've chosen
over chests of gold.
It's a ploughshare for my flesh
and an anchor for my soul.

## DAS CREUTZ

Jch habe mir das Creutz
für allem Schatz erkiest
weils meines Leibes Pflug
und Seelen Anker ist.

(4:48)

## SHREWDNESS IS PRAISED

Don't squander what you have.
A merchant's honored best
when he both has the gold
and knows how to invest.

## DIE KLUGHEIT WIRD GELOBT

Verwirff nicht was du hast:
Ein Kauffman der sein Geld
Wol anzulegen Weiss,
den lobet alle Welt.

(4:169)

## TO THE GOLD-SEEKER

O fool! You chase the world
and all the wealth of it,
not knowing that you'll fall
into a drainage pit.

## AN DEN GELD SUCHENDEN

O Narr was renstu so
nach reichthum in der Welt,
und weist doch daß man wird
dardurch inn Pful gefält?

(6:83)

## THE GATHERING OF THE
## WISE AND FOOLISH

A miser is a fool:
he gathers what will pass.
The merciful is wise:
he wants the things that last.

## WEISE UND NARRISCHE SAMMLUNG

Der Geitz-Halß ist ein Narr /
er sammlet was vergeht:
der Mild' ein weiser Mann /
er suchet was besteht.

(6:93)

# HOW THE WISE AND THE GREEDY STORE MONEY

The wise man keeps his money
wisely in a chest.
The miser? In his heart,
where it never lets him rest.

# DES WEISEN UND GEITZIGEN GELT KAMMER

Der Weiß ist klüglich reich;
er hat das Gelt im kasten /
der Geitzhalß im gemüth
drumb lästs ihn niemahls rasten.

(6:99)

## THE WISE MAN IS AHEAD
## OF THE THIEVES

The wise man does not wait
for thieves to come at will.
He treasures in himself
whatever they might steal.


## DER WEISE KOMBT DEN DIEBEN VOR

Der Weise wartet nicht
biß ihm was wird genommen:
er nihmt ihm alles selbst
den Dieben vorzukommen.

(6:100)

## THE WISE MAN HAS NOTHING
## IN HIS TREASURE CHEST

What's in the wise man's lockbox?
Nothing is.
If he can lose a thing, he thinks,
it can't be his.


## DER WEISE HAT NICHTS IM KASTEN

Ein weiser Mann hat nichts
im Kasten oder Schreyn:
Was er verlichren kan,
schätzt er nicht seine seyn.

(6:168)

## YOU MUST BE WHAT YOU
## DON'T WISH TO LOSE

The wise are what they have.
If you want to get
the pearl that's of great price,
you must turn into it.[24]

## MAN MUß SEYN WAS MAN
## NICHT VERLIHREN WIL

Der Weis' ist was er hat.
Wiltu das Feinperlein
des Himmels nicht verliehrn,
so mustu's selber seyn.

(6:169)

24. The allusion is to the parable of the pearl in Matthew 13:45–46. In the
story, a merchant finds a pearl he thinks he must have at all costs, and he sells
all he owns to buy it. The parable sets up the pearl as an image for the kingdom
of heaven: nothing is too great a sacrifice for *that*. In Angelus's hands, the pearl
becomes internal. If you want the pearl, or the kingdom of heaven, you must
become it for yourself.

## THE OUTCOME OF THE
## MISERLY AND WISE

The miser leaves his gold
to others when he's dead.
The wise man looks beyond
and sends his gold ahead.

## DER GEITZIGEN UND WEISEN WIRKUNG

Der Geitzhalß muß darvon
läst anderen sein Geld;
der Weise schickts für sich
voran in jene Welt.

(6:179)

## THE WEALTH OF THE FOOLISH AND WISE

A fool will think he's rich
with gold and nothing more.
A wise man has the world,
and thinks himself too poor.


## DER NARREN UND WEISEN SCHÄTZUNG

Der Narr hält sich vor Reich
bey einem Sak voll Geld:
Der Weise schätzt sich arm
auch bey der gantzen Welt.

(6:181)

## THE BLESSED WISE MAN

Blessed is the man[25]
who quite devotedly
spends all the time he has
upon eternity!
He looks on youth and age                  5
as if they were the Other;
he is the house of wisdom
built by God the Father.
He leans upon his staff,
the everlasting Word;                      10
he doesn't sink, like fools,
into the shifting mud.
He doesn't look for lands,
not houses, silver, gold:
he doesn't pain himself                    15
with how he shall grow old.
Blind happiness itself
can't pull him helter-skelter;
vain thirst can't drive him out
to drink forbidden water.                  20
He doesn't favor force,
he shuns all huckstering;

25. This poem, which Angelus situates near the beginning of Book 6, is a tour de force of literary themes, metaphors, and biblical allusions. The poem's opening line echoes Psalm 1 ("Blessed is the man . . ."), as does line 41 (the "Tree of Life"). Angelus includes nearly all the images he uses for wisdom and folly elsewhere in the *Cherubinic Wanderer*. Foolishness is mud, blindness, and a preoccupation with temporal things. Wisdom is a house, a path, sight, sunlight, a yearning for eternity, and a means to becoming God.

he doesn't watch himself
to see if he is seen.
To worldlings, he's a child.                    25
He knows the next town's gate
as well as any city
with a magistrate.
He looks beyond himself
as often as he can                              30
and up into the heaven,
his truer fatherland.
He doesn't reckon age
by any years that pass
but whether he grows up                         35
and into God at last.
The sun that shines so bright
upon his fields at noon
will tarry with him still
when once the day is done.                       40
He sees the Tree of Life
and yearns for it in spirit;
he takes the quickest road
to ever bring him near it.
He takes no thought for things—                 45
the world's activities
are all as clear to him
as what a blind man sees.
But he is strong and lively;
he shirks no mortal foe,                         50
not world nor flesh nor devil,
wherever he may go.
Let others chase the world
to their calamity—

*this* is the way of life,                    55
and this the path for me!

## DER SEELIGE WEISE

Wie Seelig ist der Mensch
der alle seine zeit
mit anders nichts verbringt
als mit der Ewigkeit!
Der jung und alt allein                    5
betrachtet und beschaut
der Weißheit Schloß / das Gott
sein Vater hat gebaut.
Der sich auf seinen Stab /
das ewge Wort / aufstützt                   10
und nicht wie mancher Thor
im frembden sande sitzt.
Der nicht nach Hauß und Hoff
nach Gold und Silber sieht
noch seines Lebens zeit                     15
zu zehlen sich bemüht.
Jhn wird das blinde Glük
nicht hin und her vexirn
noch etwann eitler Durst
zu frembden Wassern führn.                  20
Er weiß von keinem Zwang
er liebt nicht krämerey
er trachtet nicht darnach
daß er gesehen sey!
Er ist der Welt ein kind /                  25
die allernächste stadt
ist ihm so viel bekand

als die der Tagus hat.
Er schaut nur übersich
so frey er immer kan                                30
sein rechtes Vaterland
den lieben Himmel an.
Sein alter rechnet er
nicht nach der Jahre zahl /
in Gott vollkommen seyn                             35
das heist er Alt zumahl.
Die Sonne leuchtet ihm
in seinen Aker ein
und wenns gleich abend wird
so bleibt ihm doch ihr Schein.                      40
Er siht des Lebens Baum
im Geist begierlich an
und geht mit allem fleiß
zu ihm die nächste bahn.
Er kümmert sich umb nichts;                         45
was neben ihm geschieht
ist ihm so frembt und klar
als was ein blinder sieht.
Doch ist er stark und frisch /
er scheuet keinen Feind /                           50
wenn gleich Welt / Teuffel / Fleisch /
und mehr beisammen seind.
Ein ander lauffe hin /
zerstrew sich mit der Welt /
diß ist das Leben und die bahn                      55
so mir gefällt.

(6:11)

# Further Reading

THE FOLLOWING ARE CHRISTIAN texts that influenced Angelus Silesius. The originals were written in Greek, Latin, or German, but this list recommends good English translations for readability.

Athanasius (c. 293–373). *On the Incarnation of the Word.* Translated by Sister Penelope Lawson (C.M.S.V.), introduction by C. S. Lewis. Crestwood, NY: St. Vladimir's Seminary Press, 1996.

This text presents Athanasius's famous claim that "God became man so that man might become God"—an idea that permeates Angelus Silesius's poetry and governs his view of the soul as a wanderer on the way to union with God.

Augustine (354–430). *Confessions.* Translated by Henry Chadwick. Oxford: Oxford University Press, 1991.

Augustine recounts his intellectual journey from a naïve form of Christianity to the more attractive Gnosticism of his day, to academic skepticism after his disillusionment with Gnosticism, and to Neoplatonism after his disillusionment with skepticism, before his final return to a robust and orthodox Christianity. Along the way, he expresses many ideas that profoundly influenced later Christian thinkers. Topics include love, evil, God as the platonic Good/True/Beautiful ("Late have I loved thee, Beauty so old and so new"), and the struggle of the will in choosing between good and evil.

**Bernard of Clairvaux (1090–1153). "Sermons on the Song of Songs."
Translated by G. R. Evans in *Bernard of Clairvaux: Selected Works*. New
York: Paulist, 1987.**

Saint Bernard's teachings are often called "sweet as hon-
ey." In these sermons, Bernard preaches on the biblical
book of the Song of Solomon. He treats the book as a
love song between the human soul and God.

**Boethius (c. 476–524). *The Consolation of Philosophy*. Translated by P. G.
Walsh. Oxford: Oxford University Press, 1999.**

Written while Boethius was in prison before his behead-
ing, this book describes the soul's relationship to God as
its highest good. Boethius talks at length about the prob-
lem of evil, free will, and God's foreknowledge, arguing
not only that God is true happiness but that He is also
sovereign over earthly affairs, despite appearances to the
contrary.

**Böhme, Jakob (1575–1624). *The Way to Christ*. Translated by Peter Erb.
New York: Paulist, 1978.**

Böhme was a Lutheran shoemaker who wrote devotional
and mystical books that enjoyed widespread popularity.
Böhme had only minimal formal education and was oc-
casionally censored by local authorities, but formal in-
vestigations did not turn up serious errors. He flourished
in the decades immediately before Angelus's birth and
was likely the most direct influence on Angelus's *Cheru-
binic Wanderer*.

**Pseudo-Dionysius the Areopagite (fl. 500). *On the Divine Names* and *Mystical
Theology*. In *Pseudo Dionysius: The Complete Works*. Translated by
Colm Luibheid. New York: Paulist, 1987.**

Pseudo-Dionysius is perhaps best known for his "nega-
tive theology," in which man knows God only by knowing
what He is *not*. The unknowability of God is a recurring
theme in both Eastern and Western Christian writings,
and it influenced Angelus profoundly.

112

# Further Reading

Thomas à Kempis (c. 1380–1471). *The Imitation of Christ.* Translated by Ronald Knox and Michael Oakley. San Francisco: Ignatius, 1959.

One of the most popular and beloved books in Western history, the *Imitation* functions both as a practical handbook for Christian living and as an aid for devotion.

Thomas Aquinas (1225–1274). *Summa Theologica.* Translated by the Fathers of the English Dominican Province. Allen, TX: Thomas More, 1981.

In this massive "summary of theology," Aquinas discusses all the major questions of his day regarding the nature and actions of God. The *Summa* was foundational for Catholic theology after him, as well as for many aspects of Protestant theology. Topics include the twin roles of divine grace and human virtue in the quest for happiness, as well as theosis or the deification of the soul as it becomes united with God.

# Bibliography

Dell'Acqua, Francesca. "The Carbunculus (Red Garnet) and the Double Nature of Christ in the Early Medieval West." *Konsthistorisk tidskrift / Journal of Art History* 86.3 (2017) 158–72.

Gnädinger, Louise. *Cherubinischer Wandersmann: Kritische Ausgabe.* Ditzingen: Reclam, 1984.

Lewis, C. S. *Till We Have Faces.* New York: Harcourt Brace, 1984.

Linden, Stanton J., ed. *The Alchemy Reader.* Cambridge: Cambridge University Press, 2003.

———. *Mystical Metal of Gold: Essays on Alchemy and Renaissance Culture.* New York: AMS, 2007.

Sammons, Jeffrey L. "Johann Scheffler." In *German Baroque Writers, 1580–1660,* edited by James N. Hardin. Dictionary of Literary Biography 164. Detroit, MI: Gale, 1996.

Schuler, Robert M. *Alchemical Poetry, 1575–1700.* Routledge Library Editions: Alchemy. London: Routledge, 2013.

Shrady, Maria. *Angelus Silesius: The Cherubinic Wanderer.* New York: Paulist, 1986.

*The Table Talk of Martin Luther.* Trans. William Hazlitt. Philadelphia: Lutheran Publication Society, n.d.

# Biography of Charles Andrew Coates

This book is part of a large series from original sources of published ministry given over many years by Charles A Coates, who was born in Bradford, England, in December 1862, and died in Teignmouth, Devon in October 1945.

He relates that he started writing and publishing tracts at the age of 22, and by 1900, books collecting his lectures and writings began a limited private circulation. Interest led to more general publication of several collections included in this series. His ministry is now widely appreciated and has been frequently republished. Mr Coates may be best known for a series of Outlines of many books of the Bible. These are later than the collected tracts and lectures, being based on notes of Bible readings from 1920 up until shortly before his death, almost all of which were revised by him. A lot more of his ministry has been published since his death.

Mr Coates' ministry reflects his long life of devoted service to the Lord, and the depth and extent of his love and appreciation of divine truth. It is valued for its clarity and accessibility, and many have been drawn into the study of the Word by starting with one or other of his books. He cuts in a straight line the word of truth; not only accurate in his interpretation, but also direct and faithful in the application of the truth to our walk and conduct. He is sound on the foundations of the gospel, giving extensive guidance and assurance to souls seeking establishment in their faith.

Walter Brown sums up Mr Coates in this introduction to his published letters -

> Our brother's active service was for many years much restricted through bodily weakness, and this contributed, under the Lord's hand, to the development of ... choice spiritual feelings. His mind was remarkably formed by the teaching of the Holy Scriptures, and all that he wrote was the result of prayerful consideration. Hence the combination of unswerving faithfulness to the Lord with true humility and gracious sympathy in the spiritual experiences of others. Above all else, the reader cannot fail to remark in these pages our beloved brother's deep appreciation of the Person of Christ, and his wholehearted devotedness to His interests on earth, centring in "His body, which is the assembly". No matter affecting the Lord or His saints was regarded as too trivial for his interest and prayers, and the smallest service done for His Name and glory found recognition and appreciation.

Charles Coates was born and brought up in Yorkshire. His father, James Coates, was born in Scotland in 1809. James is said to have once been a shepherd, but from no later than 1841, he was a linen draper in Bradford. He was moved to withdraw from the Congregational Chapel there in 1846 to be among the brethren in the town; and in 1855 was married to Elizabeth Rollinson, born in nearby Otley in 1820.

Charles was converted at the age of 16 – a turning point he marked by writing the first of several hymns. Sometime before his mother died in 1905, he moved with her to Paignton, Devon. After she died, he had lodgings in Teignmouth, and lived and broke bread there until his death. He never married. Mr Coates started working with his father as a draper, but evidently gave this up -perhaps when his father died: his health was poor from an early age. His infirmity also limited how much he travelled, so that much of his ministry was either given locally, or written.

This set of books is published with the desire that others may find and get the benefit of what the Lord gave His people through our brother; and that this will be to God's glory.

D. Andrew Burr
January 2021

# CONTENTS

# THE BELIEVER ESTABLISHED
Romans 15:13

There is one thing about the epistle to the Romans which makes it differ from other epistles of Paul, and that is, the fact that, in this unfolding of the truth, he takes nothing for granted, but begins at the very foundation. When writing to the Corinthians, Galatians, Philippians, or Thessalonians, he was writing to people among whom he had labored, and we find references to what he had taught them before; and though he had not seen the Colossians, yet Epaphras had told him so much about them that he could assume they were established up to a certain point. But in writing to the Romans, he merely alludes to the fact that it was notorious in all the world that there was a company of believers at Rome. They were Gentile converts, but Paul had never seen them, and having to write a letter of commendation for Phoebe who was about to visit the imperial city, he takes the opportunity of unfolding to them "the gospel of God ... concerning his Son" from the very foundation. He will not "build upon another man's foundation"; he prefers to lay it himself, conscious of the special grace that was given to him of God: and in unfolding these foundation truths his desire was that the believers at Rome might be established according to that which he calls "*my gospel*". See Romans 1:11, Romans 16:25.

You will notice that the verse I have read in Romans 15:13, comes at the end of the doctrinal and practical part of the epistle. Many interesting personal remarks and salutations follow, but the apostle ends his teaching at this verse, and it appears to me that this is the goal to which he is aiming to conduct us through this epistle. I want to point out to you this evening the course by which this goal may be reached, but before doing so I would like you to settle it in your heart that it is the will of God that you should be filled "with all joy and peace in believing, that ye may abound in hope, through the power of the Holy Ghost". I believe if you get nothing else in this meeting but a sense in your soul, by the Spirit, that it is the will of God you should be in the condition here described, it would be an immense blessing to you, for you would go away with an exercised and longing heart, and if you hungered for them God would fill you with these good things. Have you reached this goal? Are you filled with all joy and peace in believing? Are you abounding in hope through the power of the Holy Spirit? Or have you stopped short of this blessing, into which God designs to bring you now by His Spirit? If you have not reached it I trust that the Lord will give you a word direct from Himself, that will point out the hindrance and help you over it into this wonderful blessing!

Now let us look at the course by which this goal is reached! It seems to me it is like a steeplechase or a hurdle race; that is, there are fences or barriers which have to be got over, and it is at these fences that so many are stopped in their progress and fail to reach the goal. This epistle shows us the fences, and how to get over them.

To begin with, let us suppose that a sinner – an ordinary man of the world – gets a distant view of this wonderful goal. "Filled with all joy and peace!" he says to himself, 'That must be perfect happiness! Nothing in the world has ever filled me with joy and peace. And though I do not quite understand what abounding in hope means, it sounds very nice. I must go in for these things. He sets out to run toward the goal, but very soon he is brought to a dead stand by a fence so thick and high that he may well despair of ever getting over it by his own efforts. If you want to know what it is you must read Romans 3:9 - 20.

In the first two chapters of this epistle, we find three men. In chapter 1 there is an awful portrait of a corrupt heathen who has thrown off all the restraints of natural conscience, and, turning even from the revelation of God in nature, has abandoned himself to the license of his own lusts. In the early part of chapter 2 we have a moralist, who can tell everybody what is right and wrong without being any better than others himself. In the latter part of the same chapter, we have a religious man with a Bible, and a knowledge of the true God and of His will. So that we have (1) an open profligate sinner; (2) a moralist; (3) a religious man – three men representative of every class of the unsaved – and all brought to a stand by the fence in chapter 3. No. 2 might have said to No. 1, 'I'm a much better man than you': and so he was in many respects outwardly. No. 3 might have said to No. 2, 'You do not know the true God, and you have not got His word, but I worship Him in His temple and I have His word'; and it would have been true. But all three are stopped by this terrible fence;

"ALL HAVE SINNED".

Have you ever come to this fence and found your sins standing as a terrible barrier between you and blessing? How is this awful barrier to be surmounted or removed out of the way? Will repentance do? or reformation? or prayers? or good works? or sacraments? Nay; for none of these things, nor all of them together, can atone for sins. They cannot reduce the height, or the thickness, of this dark barrier by one hair-breadth. We are utterly powerless to put away sins, therefore help must arise from another quarter or we are for ever undone. The God against whom we have sinned is the only One who can remove this great obstacle to our blessing.

"Being justified freely by his grace, through the redemption that is in Christ Jesus", Romans 3:24. Grace is the source and spring of a full and free discharge from the burden and guilt of sins. If you ask, What is *Grace*? I answer, it is the boundless love of the heart of God going out to sinners, and acting for their blessing though they deserve nothing but judgment. But divine love must be a righteous and holy love, and God would not clear away our sins in an unrighteous way. He could not make light of the guilt in which we were found, hence His grace could only reach us "through the redemption that is in Christ Jesus". A stupendous work has been done by Jesus on the cross to glorify God about sins, and believers stand before God on the ground of that work clear of every charge. It may be asked, How do we get the good of that work? Two short sentences from verses 25, 26 supply the answer – "through faith in his blood". "Him which believeth in Jesus". God justifies from every charge of guilt the one who has faith in the Person and work of Jesus.

In chapter 4, Abraham and David are brought in as illustrating the principles on which God can justify a sinner – Faith in one case and Repentence in the other. Psalm 32 shows that when the sinner *uncovers* his sins God *covers* them. "Hid" in verse 5 is the same word as "covered" in verse 1. The repenting sinner acknowledges his sin to God, and does not cover his iniquity, but confesses his transgressions unto the Lord. He makes a clean breast of every thing; in his spirit there is no guile. He condemns himself but God justifies him, and he tastes the blessedness of having his transgression forgiven, his sins covered, and righteousness imputed to him without works.

"Abraham *believed God*, and it was counted unto him for righteousness". Works have no place in connection with this matter, and boasting is excluded when we see that "a man is justified by faith without the deeds of the law", Romans 3:28. It is evident that if justification is *by grace* it must be *of faith*, "otherwise grace is no more grace", Romans 11:6. Then you will observe how the Holy

Spirit brings in the thought of God known as the God of resurrection. God was He "who quickened the dead", verse 17, and was known as such, at least in figure, by Abraham, so that "he considered not his own body, *now dead* ... neither yet the *deadness* of Sarah's womb". This leads on to the declaration that righteousness shall be imputed *to us* if we believe – not now in Jesus, but – "on him that raised up Jesus our Lord from the dead; who was delivered for our offences, and was raised again for our justification". The One who bore all our sins, and glorified God in enduring and exhausting the penalty attached to them, is clear of them all. They are entirely gone, to the perfect satisfaction of God, and the One who bore them is raised from the dead. He is in a condition where He cannot bear sins or be charged with them anymore, and the believer counted righteous by God is as clear of sins as Jesus is. It is thus that "being justified by faith, we have peace with God through our lord Jesus Christ". And while we rejoice in this, let us not forget what goes along with it. The One who bore all our sins is now as the Risen One in unclouded favor with God. He ever was, as to His own Person, the peerless Object of God's favor; but as the Risen One – the Accomplisher of redemption – He now stands in God's favor with a perfect title to set us in it also, and "by whom also we have access by faith into this grace (favor) wherein we stand, and rejoice in hope of the glory of God". The one who has entered upon this by faith has passed the first great barrier, and has made a good start towards the goal.

I remember when I got past the first fence, I thought the course would be clear right away to the goal. But it was not long before I came to another difficulty which, for two or three years, seemed to be more insurmountable than the first. It was this. I found that evil was present with me, even when I had the strongest desires to do good; and, though I longed to be holy, and devoted to Christ, I often found myself carried away captive in the grasp of sin. I made many efforts to get over this by reading the Scriptures, by prayer, by self-examination, and by resolutions and determinations. But all was in vain. There was a terrible evil within that would harass and hinder me, and throw me down in the mire in spite of all my efforts to go on to the goal. How could one be "filled with all joy and peace" while he was tormented and held in bondage by an evil power that was continually too strong for him?

From chapter 5:12 to the beginning of chapter 8 this epistle is occupied with the second fence. It is not a question of SINS, but of SIN. The matter to be considered is not our guilty actions and the way to be cleared from them, but

## OUR SINFUL SELF

and deliverance from the law of sin in our members. A certain man clings to us; go where we will he follows us; and he is continually tripping us up. If we could only run away and leave him, what a relief it would be! I have heard of a man who made up his mind to go out of the way of temptation that he might lead a perfectly holy life. So, he built a hut in the middle of a wood, took a supply of bread and a large jug of water, and sought to shut himself up where no evil could follow him. He shut the door with great delight, rejoicing to think that he had left the world and sin outside, and he was so happy that he fell on his knees to thank God that he was delivered at last. Alas! in the act of kneeling down he kicked his water jug over, and something came out of his lips which was neither thanksgiving nor prayer! With a sad and disappointed heart, he got up and went home, having made the discovery that his greatest enemy was a man from whom he could not run away.

I see that many of you quite understand an experience like that. We have to learn that as children of Adam we belong to a bad stock, and this is a very different thing from being convicted of the guilt of our sins. It is of vital importance that each young believer should learn this lesson. I do not mean as a doctrine. A theological student went to an old professor of divinity and said, 'Mr. So-and-so, I have found original sin in the Bible'. 'Have you found it in your own heart?' was the old man's reply. It is one thing to believe that the Bible says the children of Adam are a bad race; it is another to learn *by our own experience* that we belong to that race.

From the twelfth verse of Romans 5 the subject considered is that of two heads, and two races connected with those two heads. "Wherefore, as by one man sin entered into the world, and death by sin; and so, death passed upon all men, for that all have sinned ... Therefore, as by the offence of one (or, by one offence) judgment came upon all men to condemnation; even so by the righteousness of one (or, by one righteousness) the free gift came upon all men unto justification of life. For as by one man's disobedience many were made sinners so by the obedience of one shall many be made righteous". It is very solemn to consider that before Adam became the head of a race, he was a *fallen man*; he had committed an act of disobedience, the consequences of which extend to every member of his race. We are involved in the results of that act, and we learn the reality of this, as I have said, by our own experience. But over against this solemn fact is the blessed fact that God has brought in another Head. This new Head is Jesus Christ, who before He became Head accomplished a certain great act, the effect and benefit of which extends to all His spiritual race. He accomplished one great act of righteousness when He died upon the cross. We have already seen how God dealt in righteousness with our sins, but when Jesus went to the cross He was there for sin as well as for sins. See Romans 8:3. That is, He represented before God the sinful condition into which the whole race of Adam had been plunged by the fall. The only way in which God could righteously deal with that corrupt and fallen race was by closing its history in death. The race – that order of man – will not do for God, and the death of Christ is the great act of righteousness in which it has been judicially brought to an end before God, that we might be brought into blessed life and liberty in connection with another Head – Jesus Christ, the risen and exalted One. But we should have a poor and shallow idea of the meaning of this great transfer from Adam to Christ if we only learned it as a doctrine; hence it is necessary that we should learn its importance and blessedness from our own experience. Therefore, we may be sure that no person has really understood what it is to be "in Christ", or known the liberty which "the Spirit of life in Christ Jesus" confers, if he has not passed in some way through the exercises which are detailed for us in Romans 7:7 - 24.

As soon as one is born again there is a desire to be holy and to live to God, and there are more or less earnest efforts to live up to our light. It may be that the soul sets itself to keep the ten commandments; or tries to follow in the footsteps of Jesus and walk as He walked; or attempts to carry out the divine instructions given in the Christian epistles. The more intelligence of divine things that one has, the higher the standard will be to which he will seek to attain. But however sincere the desire, and however perfect and exalted the standard, the result is a total failure. The soul has to learn three things:

1. "The law is spiritual; but I am carnal, sold under sin", verse 14.

2. "If then I do that which I would not, I consent unto the law, that it is good. Now then it is no more I that do it, but sin that dwelleth in me", verses 16, 17.

3. "I know that in me (that is, in my flesh)

dwelleth no good thing", verse 18.

With a perfect standard, and an earnest desire to be up to it, he finds himself in fleshly bondage. He discovers that, in spite of all his good desires, he is so under the power of sin that he cannot be what he is honestly attempting to be. Then, further, he realizes that the sin which holds him in bondage dwells in him; and lastly, he comes to the conclusion that not only does sin dwell in him, but that as a man in the flesh there is in him *nothing but sin.* At the same time, you will notice that he learns to make a very important distinction. He finds that there is a new moral being in him which he calls "the inward man", according to which he delights in the law of God, consents to the law that it is good, and has the will to do good present with him. He identifies himself with this new moral being, and reaches the conclusion that "If then I do that which I would not ... *it is no more I that do it,* but sin that dwelleth in me". He makes a distinction between himself as born again, and sin that dwells in him. This is an important point in the soul's experience.

The next thing after learning the nature of the disease is to discover a remedy, and this the exercised one diligently attempts. He makes strenuous efforts to subjugate and restrain the evil and to promote the good, but without success. He finds a law that, when he would do good, evil is present with him; and though he delights in the law of God after the inward man, he sees another law in his members, warring against the law of his mind and bringing him into captivity to the law of sin which is in his members (verses 21 - 23). He knows the evil that is in him; he is most anxious to subdue it, but finds that he has no power. This reduced him to a state in which he can only cry, "O wretched man that I am! who shall deliver me from this body of death?" He ceases to attempt, or to look for, self-improvement. He gives himself up – that is, as a man in the flesh – as being a "body of death", and he looks for a complete deliverance out of that order of life in which he finds himself as a child of Adam.

Chapter 8, supplies us with a perfect answer to all these painful, but most necessary, exercises. If we have passed through the different stages of dissatisfaction, disappointment, disgust, and despair as to ourselves, we are ready to welcome the infinite grace that gives us title to take our place on the new ground that we are "in Christ Jesus".

We see a great deliverance effected for us by

God through Jesus Christ our Lord. We now understand the meaning and value of the statements in chapters 6 and 7, that "our old man has been crucified with him", and that we have become dead to the law by the body of Christ, that we should be married to another, even to Him who is raised from the dead, that we should bring forth fruit unto God. We are thankful to see that the death of Christ is the judicial end of our history as children of Adam; and to know that we are now entitled, and have power by the Holy Spirit, to reckon ourselves dead to sin, and alive to God in Christ Jesus.

In chapter 8, verse 1 gives us the *new position*; verse 3 shows us the righteous *ground* on which God could set us in it, and verse 2 indicates the *power* by which alone we can take, or hold, it. It is not the power of a firm resolve, or even of a fervent prayer, but the power of the Holy Spirit. You will observe that in verse 9 it is said of believers, "ye are not in the flesh, but in the Spirit, if so be that the Spirit of God dwell in you". The presence of the Holy Spirit is that which gives character to our *new state* as Christians, and when we get on to the lines on which He would lead and keep us we are in power and liberty. The one who is "in the Spirit" can say, "The law of the Spirit of life in Christ Jesus hath made me free from the law of sin and death".

We must be on the line, and in the current, of the Spirit in order to stand fast in liberty. If He has brought us to reckon ourselves dead to sin and alive to God in Christ Jesus, He would certainly ever maintain us in that reckoning. He would lead us ever to yield ourselves to God as alive from among the dead, and our members as instruments of righteousness to God. By Him we should be enabled to put to death the deeds of the body, which are only sin if it acts in virtue of its own life; and we should thus present our bodies a living sacrifice, holy and acceptable unto God, which is our reasonable service. This is the way of deliverance and liberty, and we are maintained in the power and joy of it as we walk in the Spirit. If we allow Him to control and lead us, we may be quite sure it will be on these lines. Hence these things become a practical test as to whether we are walking in the Spirit, or after the flesh. May God awaken our hearts to the immense importance and blessedness of being thus on the line of the Spirit's leading and power!

Now we must pass for a few moments to the consideration of another difficulty, which often proves a great hindrance to being filled "with all joy and peace". You will find it spoken of in Romans 8:18, as

## "THE SUFFERINGS OF
## THIS PRESENT TIME"

I have known believers who got on very happily as long as there was not a cloud in the sky, or a ripple on the wave, and to hear them talk you would suppose them to be above everything that could come to them down here. But when a touch of domestic or personal affliction comes, their confidence seems to fail. The moment squalls come they are ready to hoist a signal of distress, and sometimes wonder why God has laid such a heavy hand on them, and why they are so hardly dealt with.

Many believers are not filled with all joy and peace in believing, and are not abounding in hope through the power of the Holy Spirit, because they have not yet surmounted this third great obstacle. And depend upon it, young Christians, sooner or later you will find out that this is a time of sufferings. You may have yours in one way, and I may have mine in another, but I do not believe there is one in this company who has been quite untouched by "the sufferings of this present time". We all have them to face, but God would have us to go through them in such superiority that they should not hinder us from being "*filled* with all joy and peace".

How can this be accomplished? I think Romans 8:16 - 39, supplies the answer.

1. "The Spirit itself beareth witness with our spirit, that we are the children of God: and if children, then heirs; heirs of God, and joint heirs with Christ; if so be that we suffer with him, that we may be also glorified together". We are not dependent upon what people call Providence for the assurance of God's favor. It is not our happy circumstances and surroundings that bear witness with our spirits that we are God's children, but the Holy Spirit; and His witness cannot be disproved by any amount of "sufferings of this present time". Then, if we are children and heirs of God we are brought in, through infinite grace, to share the portion of Christ – "joint heirs with Christ".

There are two sides to this wonderful partnership with Christ – suffering with Him, and being also glorified together. Could you expect to have a better time of it in this world than Christ had? Think of what it was to Him to pass through a scene where sin had defiled and desolated everything! – where every sight and sound that met His holy eye, and fell upon His ear, told of the wreck of that fair creation over which Adam had been set as head! Ah! that blessed One tasted, as none else could taste, all "the sufferings of this present time". He knew what it was to hunger, to thirst, to spend His strength in vain and for nought, to look for comforters, and find none, to feel the bitter scorn and hatred of enemies, the more cutting treachery of His "familiar friend" in whom He trusted, and the denial and desertion of those whom He loved so well; not to speak of the unutterable burdens that pressed continually upon His heart as He "took our infirmities, and bare our sicknesses" – feeling in His Holy spirit the full weight of every disease and infirmity that He removed by His power. He was indeed, as the prophet so touchingly says, "a man of sorrows, and acquainted with grief". *He* felt everything that sin had brought into the world, and *you* have to feel something of it too. You are called to "suffer with Him". Does not that put a wonderful aspect upon all the sufferings?

2. "The sufferings of this present time are not worthy to be compared with the glory which shall be revealed to us". God has set before us a glory which so outweighs all the sufferings that no comparison can be instituted between them. He will presently bring us into a scene where everything is according to Himself; and in the meantime, while we are still linked by our mortal bodies with a creation which groans and travails

in pain, He has given us the Spirit as the First fruits and Earnest of that glory. And though we may often be encompassed with circumstances and afflictions in the midst of which we can only groan, because we know not what we should pray for as we ought, the Spirit helps our infirmities and makes intercession for us, according to God, with groanings that cannot be uttered. God has taken care that in the midst of the sufferings, and in relation to them, there should be something in our hearts by His Spirit that is perfectly according to Himself.

3. Another thing which has great power to establish our hearts as to "the sufferings of this present time" is the knowledge of the purpose of God. Read Romans 8:28 - 32. If we do *not* know what to pray for as we ought, we *do* "know that all things work together for good to them that love God, to them who are the called according to his purpose". Look at this marvelous chain of divine grace! Foreknown, predestinated, called, justified, glorified! A golden chain reaching from eternity in the past to eternity in the future, and between the two dipping down into every sorrow and every bit of suffering, turning all to good, and using all as means to the end of an eternal result in glory! So that in presence of all the sufferings we can say, "If God be for us, who can be against

us? He that spared not his own Son, but delivered him up for us all, how shall he not with him also freely give us all things?"

4. From verse 35 to the end of the chapter, every kind of trial and suffering is marshalled before us – everything that the power of evil could bring upon us is brought forward, only to establish the glorious truth that none of these things, nor all of them together, can separate the believer from the love of Christ, or from the love of God which is in Christ Jesus. So that in the face of every possible trial he can triumphantly exclaim, "*In all these things* we are more than conquerors, through him that loved us". If Paul and Silas had endured all their sufferings at Philippi *without murmuring,* they would have been conquerors. But they did more than this. They could sing in the midst of it all; they were "*more* than conquerors". They had learned that, in spite of the sufferings of this present time, they could be "filled with all joy and peace in believing", and they abounded in hope "through the power of the Holy Ghost".

There is one more great hindrance that often accounts for the fact that believers are not in this fulness of blessing; indeed, it is perhaps the most solemn and dangerous of all the hindrances that we have considered;

and that is

## CONFORMITY TO THE WORLD

"I beseech you, therefore, brethren, by the mercies of God, that ye present your bodies a living sacrifice, holy, acceptable unto God, which is your reasonable service. And be not conformed to this world: but be ye transformed by the renewing of your mind, that ye may prove what is the good, and acceptable and perfect will of God", Romans 12:1-2. Here we have the natural and proper effect of all that has gone before in this wonderful epistle coming out in practical result. These two verses are descriptive of a man who is "alive unto God". He intelligently presents his body a living sacrifice, holy, and acceptable to God. Do you not think that every effort of Satan would be put forth to hinder such a result as that? And how does he go to work? By the subtle, and generally unperceived, introduction of principles and motives that are not of God at all. The elements and principles of the world, craftily disguised and often hidden under Christian names, are brought in, and by a slow, but certain, process the believer becomes conformed to the world upon which he professes to have turned his back. Conformity to the world is the most terrible and fatal hindrance to the people of God, and has proved through long centuries the blight and ruin of the church.

Did you say in your heart, I am not much in danger of being conformed to this world? My brother, if you say so, I am afraid you are very much conformed to it already. Remember it is not so much the *outside* world that the Holy Spirit has here in view as the *inside world* – that world which a man carries in his own heart. You may wear the plainest dress, and shun everything which is outwardly known as worldliness, and yet be thoroughly conformed to this world. Allow me to suggest for your consideration that from Romans 12:1 to Romans 15:7 we may learn what it is *not* to be conformed to this world. At present I will content myself with the indication of seven particulars, which will suffice to show you that the exhortation against conformity to this world has a far deeper and more searching application than is sometimes supposed.

1. "I say, through the grace given unto me, to every man that is among you, not to think of himself more highly than he ought to think; but to think soberly, according as God hath dealt to every man the measure of faith", Romans 12:3.

2. "Mind not high things, but condescend to men of low estate", Romans 12:16.

3."Be not wise in your own conceits", Romans 12:16.

4."Dearly beloved, avenge not yourselves ... Be not overcome of evil, but overcome evil with good", Romans 12:19 - 21.

5."Let every soul be subject unto the higher powers", Romans 13:1.

6."It is high time to awake out of sleep: for now is our salvation nearer than when we believed. The night is far spent, the day is at hand", Romans 13:11,12.

7.We ought "not to please ourselves. Let every one of us please his neighbor for his good to edification. For even Christ pleased not himself", Romans 15:1 - 3.

I commend these seven particulars, and the whole of the chapters from which they are taken, to your prayerful consideration, as I believe it is only so far as these lovely traits are found in us that we are "not conformed to this world". You will observe that all the points have to do with the state and condition of our mind, rather than with anything that is outward. Hence the exhortation is, "Be ye transformed by the renewing of your mind". Depend upon it, if there is this inward renewing, it will bring a great change over our whole appearance and deportment, but the transformation must begin *within*. One thing I am sure of, that you will neither be filled with all joy and peace through believing, nor will you abound in hope through the power of the Holy Spirit, if you are conformed to this world.

Now we come to what I have called the goal of the epistle. The believer who has peace and deliverance, who is more than conqueror in all the sufferings of this present time, and who is not filled to this world, must and will be filled "with all joy and peace in believing". Then you cannot help noticing that all through the epistle the result of God's grace is to put the believer in a condition of *Hope*. When he is justified and has peace with God he rejoices "*in hope* of the glory of God". Then in chapter 8, when he is in spiritual liberty, he still has a body connected with the old creation, and he looks for the moment when God will quicken that mortal body by His Spirit, he waits for the adoption, to wit, the redemption of his body; he is saved *in hope*; his salvation is nearer day by day than when he believed. In a world of God's enemies, and in a creation, which is blighted by sin, the believer must be in a condition of hope. He cannot make himself at home in such circumstances. But in this condition of *hope* he finds himself thoroughly at one with God, who reveals Himself as "the God of hope". God puts Himself alongside us in this condition of hope into which His grace has brought us, for He is hoping too. He is looking forward to that day of glory which will display in full splendor the counsels of His grace, and He would have us in communion with the expectancy of His own heart. He would fill us with all joy and peace in believing, that we might *abound in hope* through the power of the Holy Spirit. That is, He would give us now, by faith and in the Spirit's power, such a full portion of heavenly joy and peace in our hearts that every link with the present order of things would be broken, and our souls would be filled with bright anticipation of that glory, in which our surroundings and our bodily condition will be in perfect harmony with the joy and peace that fill our hearts. We should thus "abound in hope, through the power of the Holy Ghost". This would be the effect of Paul's gospel, if we were established in it, and there is One who is of power to establish us according to that gospel. May this full blessing be the enjoyed portion of each one in this company! May God bless and establish each one of us, to the glory of His Son Jesus Christ our Lord!

———————

# THREE SCENES OF JUDGMENT
## Genesis 22:1-14 Genesis 21:8-14
## Genesis 19:27-28

These scriptures bring before us Three Scenes of Judgment, and I would like to say a few words about them, looking to the Lord that He may graciously use what comes before us for the help and blessing of the many young believers present. On each of the three occasions you will notice that Abraham rose up "early in the morning". He was a man in earnest – a man with purpose of heart. Faith was in lively and vigorous exercise. No love of selfish case, no supine and carnal indulgence, retarded his movements. He was a man in the energy of *faith*. My brethren, it is in proportion as this marks us that we shall get blessing from God. If our hearts are awake to the reality and blessedness of divine things, and we are set upon them, I am sure we shall be greatly enriched with spiritual blessing and joy.

In these chapters the man who is in the energy of faith witnesses three scenes of judgment, and it is of great importance that we should realize the typical significance of the pictures thus brought before us, for we cannot have peace without seeing the first, we shall not have joy unless we see the second, and our testimony will be a total failure if we do not see the third.

There is no type in Scripture more expressive than this touching scene in Genesis 22. Though the uplifted hand was stayed, and the fatal blow did not actually fall, the picture is so plain in its outlines that he who runs may read its meaning. It brings before us the greatest of all facts – that God "spared not his own Son, but delivered him up for us all", Romans 8:32. Mark the words, "delivered him up"! Other scriptures tell us that He gave Him, that He sent Him, that He anointed Him, that He was with Him; but the supreme fact brought before us in the type we are considering is that He delivered Him up. It is not the incarnation that is thus spoken of, for as incarnate the Holy One of God could say, "Thou keptest me in safety when I was upon my mother's breasts", Psalm 22:9, margin. Nor was He "delivered up" during His holy life of devoted service here, for again and again are we told that His enemies could not take or touch Him because "his hour was not yet come". But there came a moment when, in view of the cross and of all that was to be accomplished there, He was "delivered unto the Gentiles", Luke 18:31,32.

While we consider this, let us not forget that, if delivered up, He also "gave himself". The true Isaac was in perfect accord with all the thoughts of God which necessitated His being delivered up. The words are twice repeated in Genesis 22, "they went *both of them together*", and in the deepest way was this true of God and His beloved Son as They moved on together in that wondrous path of divine love which ended at the cross. In that path the Son could say, "He that sent me is with me: the Father hath not left me alone; for I do always those things that please him", John 8:29. I want your eyes and hearts to be fastened on that true Isaac, delivered up and giving Himself on the cross, where we see

## THE SON OF GOD UNDER JUDGMENT

Two things made Calvary's scene of judgment necessary, if sinners were to be brought into blessing. First, the *holiness of God* demanded that there should be judgment upon sin. If the holy Sufferer cries, in the anguish of His soul, "My God, my God why hast thou forsaken me?" He supplies the answer to that unparalleled enquiry by saying, "*But thou art holy*, O thou that inhabitest the praises of Israel", Psalm 22:1 - 3. And, in the second place, *an awakened conscience* could never have peace in the presence of

God, apart from the knowledge of the fact that sin has been dealt with in righteous and holy judgment. Have you got peace? Can you say, before God, 'There is not a cloud above, and not a spot within'? If not, may this be the hour of your introduction into this priceless blessing! I purpose to bring briefly before you four aspects of the infinite work of the Son of God upon the cross.

1. "Jesus our Lord ... who was delivered for our offences, and was raised again for our justification", Romans 4:25. God has provided a Person capable of bearing sins and their judgment in such a way that the holiness of God, instead of being against the sinner who believes, is absolutely in his favour. We see at the cross the infinite holiness of God in His judgment of our sins; but we see that judgment failing upon One who bears it in voluntary self-sacrifice and devoted love, in order that we may be justified and have Peace with God. He gave Himself for our sins, bearing them in His own body on the tree, and by Himself He purged them. Has He removed them all? Certainly! If you remember who He was, you can have no question as to the value and efficacy of His work. If any great work has to be done, satisfaction and confidence as to it are based upon knowing the competency of the person engaged in it. Think of the

glory of the Person who was "delivered for our offences"! What failure can there be in a work undertaken by the Son of God? After *such a* Person has done *such a* work God can say righteously about the sins of believers, "Their sins and iniquities will I remember no more", Hebrews 10:17.

God has "raised up Jesus our Lord from the dead". Our Savior is clean out of the death and judgment that He went into "for our offences", and in God's account every believer is as clear as He is. Knowing this, we are justified by faith, and "have peace with God through our Lord Jesus Christ", Romans 5:1.

2. "For what the law could not do, in that it was weak through the flesh, God sending his own Son in the likeness of sinful flesh, and for sin, condemned sin in the flesh", Romans 8:3. The truth contained in this verse has to do with what *we are,* and not with what we *have done.* We should all be prepared to admit that we have done many wrong things, but this outflow of evil must have had a *source.* So much bad fruit could never have been produced by a good tree. What *we have done* is the outcome of what *we are.* Now, as to this, it is written, "I know that *in me* (that is, in my flesh) dwelleth *no good thing*", Romans 7:18. The Scriptures

declare this, and sooner or later, the experience of every converted person will confirm it. I remember a young man saying to me, after some days of deep exercise on what seemed likely to be his death-bed, 'The Lord has been showing me what I am. I knew before that there was a lot of *bad* in me, but I never saw until now that there is *no good*'. This is a very solemn but needful lesson.

The very existence of "sinful flesh" was a great dishonour to God. That man – the special object of God's heart – should be found in a condition of sin, and in such a state that for the eye of God there is in him "no good thing", is an appalling fact. What could be done with "sinful flesh" for God's credit and glory? The material was too bad for any remedy to be successful. The law might be applied to it, and might detect the evil, but could neither put it right nor remove it to the glory of God. The verse I have read shows how God has dealt with sinful flesh. He has condemned sin in the flesh, and made an end to it in the death of His Son. The man in whom no good dwells was ended before God in the death of Christ. Sinful flesh has been removed in judgment from before God at the cross.

3. "Forasmuch then as the children are

partakers of flesh and blood, he also himself likewise took part of the same; that through death he might destroy him that had the power of death, that is, the devil; and deliver them who through fear of death were all their lifetime subject to bondage", Hebrews 2:14,15. The devil has no power beyond death – not even over the lost. People get hold of fictitious poetical ideas, and picture him reigning over an infernal kingdom beyond death; but in truth the devil will be forever the most abject of all lost creatures. His kingdom is bounded by the grave; his territories stretch down to death, but there they end. God allowed the devil to have the power of death, and to wield it in a reign of terror over the consciences of men. Idolatry, superstition, and priestcraft exercise their dark tyranny over more than a thousand million, of the human race, and the secret of their dominion is the fear of death, with the power of the devil behind it.

Then again, when the conscience of a sinner is awakened by the Spirit of God, the fear of death lays the soul in heavy irons and cruel bondage. I expect that most, if not all, of us here have known something of this. There is a terrible reality in death. It is a dark, black cloud which comes over everything that we have and are as children of Adam. It is the blighting of every natural hope, and the desolation of every earthly prospect. It is the complete break-up of our whole status as in the flesh. If ever the true thought of what death is has come home to you, you know right well that it filled your conscience with solemn fear. There is but one way of deliverance from the fear of death, and that is by the knowledge of this precious Savior, who went into death for us. Jesus has tasted death in all its bitterness and reality as the wages of sin, the power of the devil, and the judgment of God. He has entered into it fully, as none other ever could, that He might deliver us forever from its fear. He has gone under all that power of darkness, that He might annul it for you and me.

Satan cannot touch that which survives death. If you become possessed of that which is on the other side of death, you have that which Satan cannot touch. Thank God! Jesus is risen. It is a Savior who has been into death for us, but is now for ever beyond it, who is the righteousness, life, and joy of the believer. All our blessings are in One who is beyond death. These are the "*sure mercies*" (Acts 13:34), and there are no other *sure* mercies. You may lose your money, your position, your abilities, your friends, your health; indeed, there is nothing *sure* this side of death, but everything is sure that is on the other side. Nothing can fail or break down that we have in a risen Savior.

4. "Walk in love, as Christ also hath loved us, and hath given himself for us an offering and a sacrifice to God for a sweet-smelling savour", Ephesians 5.2. I have read this scripture that we may not lose sight of the infinite preciousness of the work of Christ *to God*. He was under judgment and in death, but He was there for the glory of God, and there in the perfections of divine affections. His devotedness to God, and His love to the Father, were never so expressed as when He gave Himself for us. He brought the obedience and affections of the SON into the place of sin, and judgment, and death, and this made His work an offering and a sacrifice of "sweet-smelling savor".

> *"Love that on death's dark vale*
> *Its sweetest odors spread;*
> *Where sin o'er all seemed to prevail,*
> *Redemption's glory shed".*

The true Isaac has been offered up, and by His death sins have been purged, sin in the flesh has been condemned, the power of the devil annulled, the believer perfected forever, and God glorified. Perfect assurance and peace must be the portion of everyone who looks by faith on that scene of holy judgment, and learns that everything has been settled thus according to the glory of

God. In view of that scene, and of the risen Savior, who is now triumphantly out of it, darkness, doubt, and fear are banished from the heart, and the conscience is filled with perfect peace.

We may now turn to Genesis 21, and I think we shall have no difficulty in recognizing that the picture presented to us, in the expulsion of Ishmael from Abraham's house, is that of

## THE FLESH UNDER JUDGMENT

We have already seen how sinful flesh has come under the judgment of God at the cross, and if we really know this, we shall see that of necessity the flesh must also be a judged thing with the believer. It is impossible to think that God, having condemned sin in the flesh in the death of His Son, will tolerate the flesh in a believer. And it is monstrous to suppose that a believer can rejoice to know that the flesh has been judged at the cross, and be content to tolerate or gratify it in himself. But, as a matter of fact, we have to learn what the flesh is, and to discover by our own experience the utter impossibility of getting any good out of it, before we are prepared to disown it. The incorrigible badness of Ishmael had to be proved before Abraham was prepared to expel him. And it is of the deepest importance to note well the fact that it was the presence and the honoring of Isaac which brought Ishmael out in his true colors, as not having a single thought in common with God.

Ishmael had been fourteen years in Abraham's house when God brought Isaac into the house, and the introduction of Isaac was a plain declaration that Ishmael would not do for God. He was the child of nature, and none but the child of promise – the child of resurrection power – would do for God. But Ishmael did not see this. I dare say he thought he was quite as worthy to be the heir of the promises as the newcomer, to say nothing of his priority of fourteen years. Why Abraham and Abraham's God were not satisfied with him he could not make out, for he was very well satisfied with himself. He did not see the need of another man. He was mortified at being set aside by the newcomer, for it was evident that if Isaac was to increase, Ishmael must decrease. If Isaac was to be *everything*, it would make *nothing* of Ishmael, which was simply intolerable. He mocked! His true character came out – he had not a thought in common with God. Ishmael is a type of man after the flesh, Isaac is a type of man according to the promise and purpose of God, *i.e.,* of christ.

Let me seek to show you the bearing of

this, first of all, in a dispensational way. God tried man in the flesh in all kinds of circumstances, and with all kinds of privileges and advantages, for four thousand years, without ever getting any satisfaction in him. The whole history of man, as we have it in Scripture, serves to prove that man in the flesh is a moral wreck, and a grief and dishonor to God. At the end of four thousand years God brought in the promised Seed – the One in whom His heart could rest, and in whom all His promises and purposes could be established. What was the effect? The presence of Isaac brought out the true character of Ishmael. There were venerable men in Judæa – men deeply read in the oracles of God – praying men – men entirely given up to the cultivation of their own sanctity and religious character, and *these men* were the haters and rejecters – the betrayers and murderers – of Christ.

It was not the profane multitude who sought the death of Christ, but the educated, the religious, the priestly class. It was a man in the flesh *in his best form* that hated Christ. And why? I think we might say the Lord Jesus was marked for death in the minds of these religious men from the moment that He said, "I say unto you, that except your righteousness shall exceed the righteousness of the scribes and Pharisees, ye shall in no case enter into the kingdom of heaven", Matthew 5:20. A word like that swept away at once as worthless the whole fabric of the righteousness which these men had with patient toil been rearing for themselves. It made *nothing* of their prayers and religious duties; it poured contempt on all their ceremonies and observances; it reduced them to the level of common sinners, and, in short, it declared plainly that Ishmael – man in the flesh – would not do for God, however good and religious he might pretend to be. Christ was guilty in their eyes of the unpardonable offence of making nothing of all their pretensions; and on this account they hated Him with a vindictiveness which pursued Him to the cross. Ishmael would not give place to Isaac.

Nor are religious people different at the present day. If you tell those who are doing their best to be good, and working hard to elevate man, that all their efforts are useless, and that not one bit of man's goodness, or one scrap of his righteousness, will ever be accepted by God, that nothing but Christ will do for God, and that they must have Him as their righteousness and life, or be for ever lost – they will mock as scornfully as did Ishmael. Ishmael would not mind Isaac having a share; perhaps he would not object to Isaac coming to teach him, or to set him a good example; but for Isaac to be everything, so that Ishmael must be nothing, is unendurable.

But let us bring the matter a little more closely home. Ishmael is not far from any of us, and it is of vital importance to our spiritual prosperity and joy that we should know him, and deal with him as he deserves. One of our greatest snares is the pretension of the flesh to be good. In the experience of Romans 7 our souls learn what the flesh is in its native badness, as opposing all the good and holy desires of the inward man – it is there Ishmael with a dirty face. But in Galatians we see the flesh posing in quite another character. It is Ishmael with his face washed, and professing to be very good indeed. He has turned over a new leaf and quite altered his ways, and now he will be as holy as you please. He will be circumcised, he will keep the law, he will observe days, and months, and times, and years, he will fast and pray, and will endeavor to be a model Christian. He is prepared to do anything if you will only be so kind as not to ignore him altogether. Allow him to have a place – recognize him as having some status in the house, and he will be your most humble servant! In plain words, SELF is ever seeking to have a place and to be something; but this can only be at the expense of Christ and of the true joy of a Christian. Ishmael must be cast out.

Our self-importance is our greatest hindrance: it shuts Christ out. Every bit of Christ that comes into your soul makes less of *you*. If you are not prepared to give up Ishmael, you will make no spiritual progress. A man who is self-sufficient, and who wants to have credit for *himself*, is not honoring Isaac. He may preach or pray, and be very well pleased with himself when he has done it, especially if he thinks he has made an impression. This is all Ishmael – the man who will not do for God. As a Christian gets on in his soul, and as Christ becomes more to his heart, he does not think of himself or of his own glory at all, and then what he does is in the power of the Spirit of God. If you are not prepared to give your own importance, all the reading and bearing in the world will not help you much in your spiritual life. People try to make their Christianity a distinction to themselves: and this is only Ishmael – the man that will not do for God.

If nothing but Christ will do for God, all that I am must go. I may set to work to make myself as pious as possible; after the straightest sect of my religion I may live a Pharisee, and all this in thorough earnestness and sincerity: but it will not do for God. *Death* is upon all my moral, mental, and physical powers as a child of Adam – they can yield nothing for God. There must be another Man! I trust that Isaac has come to your house! You can say, 'Thank God! I know and have Christ as my Savior'. But have you yet celebrated the 'great feast'? I am persuaded that you will not have true Christian joy until you do. There are many believers who have got Isaac in the house but have not celebrated the feast. There came a day when Abraham would declare unmistakably that Isaac was the heir, not Ishmael. The "great feast" was the declaration that Isaac was the one to whom belonged all the rights of the house. Have *you* celebrated such a feast in your soul's history? Have you acknowledged with gladness of heart that nothing counts with God but Christ? that the best bit of self in you is hateful to God? Are you *glad* to know that it is only as Christ lives in you that there is anything for God? Do you refuse to tolerate, or gratify, or acknowledge the flesh, because you have learnt that it is entirely opposed to what is of God? Have you cast Ishmael out?

At this point I would like to bring before you two simple illustrations of the way in which self is displaced in the heart of the believer. When David returned from the slaughter of the Philistine, and was brought before Saul with the head of Goliath in his hand, we are told that "it came to pass, when he had made an end of speaking unto Saul, that the soul of Jonathan was knit with the soul of David, and Jonathan loved him as his own soul ... And Jonathan stripped himself of the robe that was upon him, and gave it to David, and his garments, even to his sword, and to his bow, and to his girdle", 1 Samuel 18:1,4. Jonathan had been, in figure under the power of death, but had been freed by David's victory. His heart was now at leisure to admire, and delight itself in, the lovely *grace of the victor*. The personal grace of the one who stood there with such a perfect absence of self-consciousness and self-elation, whose whole demeanor showed that he had no motive but the glory of the living God in undertaking such a conflict, won his heart so that he could ignore himself. In presence of the lovely grace of David he found pleasure in *stripping himself*. Naturally, he might have been vexed and mortified that another should have the honors of the day; but the one who had all the honors had also all the affections of his heart, and this made all the difference. The natural man hates the one who supersedes him, but the believer's heart is knit to him. Christ has stripped Himself for the glory of God, and for our deliverance and salvation.

Such is His grace. He has given Himself. Is it not enough to knit the heart of any Jonathan to the true David, and to so move and win his affections that he will rejoice to ignore himself? It is thus that we celebrate the feast, and that Ishmael is cast out.

You may see the same thing in the woman of Luke 7. The grace of the Person before her heart made her forget herself altogether. She was happy to be at His feet – to make nothing of herself in His presence – and she was heedless of all that might be thought or said of *her*. Isaac had his true place in her heart, and Ishmael was unthought of. In the presence of Christ, and only there, we recognize the worthlessness of flesh, and are able to ignore self. This is the way the Spirit of God works to produce true holiness. It is by leading our *hearts* into deepening acquaintance with Christ, and into the knowledge of the divine satisfaction which God has found so perfectly in Him.

There is one scene above all others where the worthlessness of Ishmael and the surpassing excellence of Isaac are fully displayed together. It is brought to view in these words of Paul: "For the love of Christ constraineth us; because we thus judge, that if one died for all, then were all dead: and that he died for all, that they which live should not henceforth live unto themselves, but unto him which died for them, and rose again", 2 Corinthians 5:14, 15. Here we see plainly that the judgment of death is upon every power and faculty of man; yea, upon man himself. "*All dead*" is the solemn judgment of God passed on man at Calvary. But wondrous love is there as well as holy judgment. How it touches the heart!

For me – a worthless sinner under the judgment of God, yet withal a proud, self-righteous, and self-sufficient sinner – Christ has died. There is no love like that. It surpasses all illustrations; it baffles description. If I gaze on that scene, I learn *my* utter worthlessness and unfitness for God, but I find *love* there that wins my heart. *In presence of that love*, I can only be nothing, and I am happy to be nothing. Ishmael is displaced from my affections, and Isaac is enthroned there.

Paul could say, "I am crucified with Christ: nevertheless I live; yet not I, but Christ liveth in me: and the life which I now live in the flesh I live by the faith of the Son of God, who loved me, and gave himself for me", Galatians 2:20. To observe legal ordinances and to keep up ceremonial distinctions might be an object to others – *they* might wish to retain Ishmael: but the motive object of Paul's life was a Person whose love to Paul had carried Him unto death, and that Person the Son of God. How "weak and beggarly" to use the emphatic words of the Holy Spirit – every legal and self-righteous motive becomes, when contrasted with such an object! The effect is that we are so attracted by the grace, beauty, and perfection of Christ, that it is the deepest joy to know that He is our life, and that He is in us by the Spirit. When we recognise this by the Holy Spirit, Ishmael is turned out. That is, we "rejoice in Christ Jesus, and *have no confidence in the flesh*", Philippians 3:3.

The Scripture says, "They that are Christ's have crucified the flesh with the affections and lusts", Galatians 5:24. God judged the flesh at the cross, and He has given us His Spirit that we might be of one mind with Him about it. May we have grace, my brethren, to disown, and to regard as a judged thing the flesh in every aspect! There is self-indulgent and worldly flesh, there is flesh that is consequential and obtrusive; but there is flesh that is pious, particular, and orthodox – flesh that is anxious to have the character of being lowly, earnest, devoted, intelligent, and unselfish. In every phase of his character may Ishmael be kept under judgment by each one of us!

The question may be asked, But, if turned out, does he not return? Yes, if Isaac loses his place. Just as soon as Christ ceases to command our affections the flesh in some form gets a footing. There is no middle ground between walking in the Spirit and walking after the flesh. If I am doing the first, Christ is before me: I am in the affections and liberty of sonship; my desires and motives are those which are suitable to God; and the fruit of the Spirit is developed in me. But when I drop out of the current of the Spirit by departing from grace, by lack of dependence (or by indifference to Christ,) I throw the door open for Ishmael; and I am then controlled, not by Christ and the Spirit, but by rules and restrictions to which I submit myself in order that my character may not suffer. *Nothing but the present power of divine affections* in our hearts by the Spirit can keep Ishmael out.

I must now turn for a few moments to the third scene to which I have referred, and we shall find that it is a picture of

THE WORLD UNDER JUDGMENT.

From the mountain-top "where he stood before the Lord", Abraham "looked toward Sodom and Gomorrah, and toward all the land of the plain, and beheld and, lo, the smoke of the country went up as the smoke of a furnace", Genesis 19:27, 28. Sodom and Gomorrah are typical of the world, and the man of faith sees them under the judgment of God. I do not believe there can be any true testimony for Christ unless we see that the world is under judgment.

It is a wonderful and a fascinating scene that is around us. Whether your natural tastes are low or elevated – sensual or refined – there is that in the world which perfectly answers to them. Vanity Fair presents an endless diversity of things. You may have self-gratification and self-display in things mechanical, commercial, intellectual, political, social, scientific, artistic, or religious! And the devil is at the head of the whole system – the invisible organizer and manager of the whole order of things which is "not of the Father, but is of the world". It is the whole circle of things in which men live and move *at a distance from God.*

Of course, God views the world not as a material, but as a moral, system. It is made up of lust, self-gratification, and vanity. "All that is in the world" comes under three heads: (1) The lust of the flesh; (2) The lust of the eyes; (3) The pride of life. 1 John 2:16. There is no room for the Son of the Father in such a circle, and His rejection has manifested that "now is the judgment of this world", John 12:31.

And Scripture assures us that the judgment of God will soon fall in actual fact upon the world. The book of the Revelation brings before us "things which must shortly come to pass". Are they fancies or fictions? Nay, they are tremendous realities! And everything which will actually fall under God's judgment *then is* morally under it *this minute.* Is not this very solemn? We would not like to have a link with the world in the day when the fire of God shall stream down to blast it with eternal destruction. But what about today? Is the world better now than it will be then?

"Love not the world", says the Holy Spirit. Beware of the first turning of the heart in that direction. Achan coveted the goodly Babylonish garment, and the silver and gold, and *hid* them in his tent. Backsliding often begins thus. Something of the world is cherished *in secret.* The heart finds enjoyment in something which it would not like to be known. Reading a book, perhaps, that is carefully put out of sight if any godly Christian is expected to call. "Is there any secret thing with thee?"

I do not think that talking and preaching are necessarily testimony. I believe separation from the world is essential to

Christian testimony. I do not mean by this an outward separation from certain things that we choose to designate as *worldly*, but having our affections so in the things of the Father and of the Spirit, that the motives and desires which rule in "the world" have no place in our hearts.

If I am controlled and colored by the same motives and desires as a man of the world, I shall have no more power for testimony before him than Lot in Sodom. If we are keeping the "great feast" and Christ reigns in our affections, it will be the language of our hearts to say with Paul, "God forbid that I should glory, save in the cross of our Lord Jesus Christ, whereby the world is crucified unto me and I unto the world". Galatians 6:14.

May the truths typified by these Three Scenes of Judgment have such a place in our souls that each one of us may have unclouded peace and joy, and be found in distinct testimony for the One who is rejected by the world!

———————

# ADAM OR CHRIST

I have no greater joy than to see a company like this of young believers, found together with a desire to know more of the Lord, and to be more devoted to Him in this world. I feel very dependent on the Lord that He may help me to say a few words that will help you.

I should like to bring before you the simple but most important fact that the whole of Scripture is the history of two men – Adam and Christ – and I want briefly to show you several ways in which God sets Adam aside and brings in Christ.

The moment that Adam sinned, God's satisfaction in him came to an end. Instead of innocence, the germs of all possible evil were found in his heart, and he became subject to the judgment of God. The full fruit of sin did not come out in Adam personally; it has taken the whole history of the world to develop and exhibit it; but every bit of evil that has ever come out in Adam's children was latent in him as soon as he became a sinner. I will ask you to read four scriptures which show the true character of fallen man, that is of Adam, Genesis 6:5, 6; Psalm 14:2, 3; Mark 7:20 - 23; Acts 7:51, 52.

These scriptures give us God's estimate of the children of Adam at four great periods of their history. When man is allowed to take his own course, as in antediluvian times, every imagination of the thoughts of his heart is only evil continually; when checked and restrained by God's government, as in the time of David, there are none that seek God or that do good; when His beloved Son comes to manifest all God's grace, He finds man's heart the same fruitful source of evil as ever; and the awful climax of the dark history is the betrayal and murder of the only Just One, and the perpetual resistance of the Holy Spirit. What a history! And every bit of it, and every bit of sin that you and I have found in the depths of our own hearts, is just the exhibition of that one man – Adam. It may be all summed up in a word of three letters – sin.

It is very evident that God could neither find satisfaction in, nor bring in blessing through, a man like that – a man whose every motive and activity only presents some phase of *sin*. If blessing is brought in from God it must be *through* and *in* another Man. I think you will see plainly how Adam is set aside and Christ brought in

## PROPHETICALLY
### in the Old Testament.

Two or three scriptures will indicate what I mean, and you can trace out the subject more fully for yourselves. Genesis 3:15; Galatians 3:16; Isaiah 11:1; 49: 6. It is most interesting in reading the Old Testament to find that, from Genesis 3 onwards, every blessing that God speaks of is connected with a coming Man. It was the Seed of the woman who was to bruise the serpent's head; it was in that one Seed of Abraham that all the nations were to be blessed; the Rod out of the stem of Jesse and the Branch out of his roots alone could bring in millennial righteousness and peace; He alone could be given for a light to the Gentiles, and to be God's salvation to the end of the earth. All through the Old Testament we see that every blessing, whether for Israel or for the Gentiles, was to be brought in by a coming Man. Blessing was to come, not in, or through, *Adam* and his race, but in, and through Christ.

Then, if we turn to the New Testament, we find the long-promised One here upon earth, presenting to God a perfect contrast to "the children of men", and filling God's heart with satisfaction, so that we may say that Adam was superseded by the presence of Christ on earth.

I want you to call back to your minds for a moment the four scriptures descriptive of the children of Adam which we looked at a few moments ago, and contrast them with these wonderful words, *"In thee I am well pleased"*, Luke 3:21, 22. If, on the one hand, God had looked in vain to find one atom of good in Adam personally, or in his race, on the other He could now gaze with infinite complacency upon a Man who filled His heart with delight. What a moment it was for God! With what relief, may we not say, did God's eye turn from the desolate waste of sinful humanity to that one peerless Object! In the actual history of the world, there was a Man here filling God's heart with pleasure – One who had taken part in flesh and blood, and come into all the circumstances and responsibilities of man, that He might be found in those circumstances, and under those responsibilities, as the absolutely perfect Object of God's delight. There was now a Man worthy of the opened heavens and the Father's salutation as His "beloved Son". Contrast that One with Adam – with yourself – and say whether the One is not as worthy to be the Object of God's delight, as the other is deserving of His judgment?

I will give you two portraits to look at. Here they are –

| Romans 3 | Matthew 5 |
|---|---|
| 1. "There is no fear of God before their eyes" | 1. "Blessed are the poor in spirit". |
| 2. "The poison of asps is under their lips" | 2. "Blessed are they that mourn". |
| 3. "Whose mouth is full of cursing and bitterness" | 3. "Blessed are the meek". |
| 4. "There is none righteous, no, not one: there is none that understandeth, there is none that seeketh after God" | 4. "Blessed are they which do hunger and thirst after righteousness". |
| 5. "Their feet are swift to shed blood" | 5. "Blessed are the merciful". |
| 6. "Their throat is an open sepulchre" | 6. "Blessed are the pure in heart". |
| 7. "Destruction and misery are in their ways: and the way of peace have they not known" | 7. "Blessed are the peacemakers". |

One of these portraits is Adam – or, in another word, *yourself* – and the other is Christ. Compare the dark and ugly features of the one with the fair, heavenly beauty of the other, and tell me which you prefer! Will you not say with an enraptured heart, "Thou art fairer than the children of men!" That is really to say, 'I prefer Christ to myself'. It is a grand moment in the soul's history when that point is reached, and immense issues hang upon it. But before going further with this, I must say a few words on another subject which has an important bearing on what is before us.

Before anyone can really see, or enter, into

divine things he must be born again. There is no capacity in the child of Adam, as such, to enter into the thoughts of God. If he is to be brought into touch with God, there must be a new moral being formed in him, so that we may say that Adam is set aside

MORALLY
by the new birth.

I know that I am speaking to those who believe in the absolute necessity of the new birth. Indeed, John 3:3 - 6, leaves no room for hesitation as to this on the part of any who believe the Scriptures. But have you really considered why the new birth is so absolutely necessary? A simple illustration may serve to point us to the answer! I had to see about some work being done the other day, and was asking the contractor how much it would cost. 'It won't cost very much', said he, *because we can use all the old material*. Now that is precisely what God *could not* do. There must be a new start altogether with new material. The child of Adam, as such, breaks God's law and despises God's grace; divine love fails to reach his heart, and divine light upon his conscience only drives him behind the trees of the garden, as in Eden, or away from its searching scrutiny, as in John 8. If there is to be anything *for God* in man, or any capacity to estimate things according to God, a man "must be born again". There must be an effectual operation of God by His word and Spirit producing a new moral being in man, the effect of which is that he begins to think God's thoughts about himself. God rejects the old material altogether and begins entirely anew, and the one who is born again begins to learn the true character of the old material – i.e., all that he is as a child of Adam and a man in the flesh – and to be as dissatisfied with it as God is. You may see this in Job and Saul of Tarsus. One of them said, "I abhor myself", and the other said, "I know that in me (that is, in my flesh) dwelleth no good thing". Such language as this is the mark of one born again. He identifies himself with that new "inward man" which is of God, and he judges everything of a contrary nature to be *sin*. In itself this is not a happy experience. It is not very pleasant for one who has been self-sustained and self-satisfied in a moral and religious life to find that there is not one bit of good in him. Some may discover this by a single flash of divine light, as in the case of Saul of Tarsus, and others may have years of struggling and disappointment before they learn it, but it must, and will, be learned sooner or later by every one that is born again.

If not very pleasant it is very needful, that

we should be made to cry, "O wretched man that I am!" for only thus are we truly prepared to drop ourselves and rejoice in all the grace that comes to us through and in Christ. Some people seem to get as far as being dissatisfied with themselves, and there they stick in the mud. There is something wrong if you stick there year after year groaning over your own badness. God would bring you to judge yourself, but He would not keep you there, and I should be glad if He gave you a push off that mud-bank tonight. He wants you to have the gladness of knowing that you are in the favor and acceptance of Christ, the risen and glorified Man. God would not give you anything less than this, and you could not desire anything more. God would have the faith and affection of your heart turned from yourself to Him – from Adam to Christ. If you are disgusted with yourself, you will be glad to know that you are entitled to give yourself up altogether, and enter upon the new ground that Christ is everything for you, and that you are in all His acceptance with God. But in order to do this, the work of the cross must be known, and that brings me to the next part of my subject. You have to learn that the first man, Adam, has been set aside

JUDICIALLY,
in the death of Christ.

If God has let you down, with His candle in your hand, into the dark recesses of your being as a child of Adam, to find that there is nothing there but sin, you cannot rest until you know that it has all been taken into account and dealt with to His perfect satisfaction. The cross of Christ shows you how God could provide for His own glory while taking into consideration everything that you are. God has not overlooked, or ignored, the sinful state in which you find yourself as a child of Adam. He has had it brought before Him, and it has received its full condemnation, and is removed judicially from His sight for ever. I said, a few minutes ago, that the whole character of Adam and of his children was summed up in three letters – S, I, N. When the One who knew no sin went to the cross, He was *made sin* for us, 2 Corinthians 5:21. The Holy One of God was upon that cross "*for sin*" (Romans 8:3), so that when He hung there all the sin that is in you was brought before God, for He was your Representative. Having taken such a place in deep, divine love, all the desert and consequence of *sin* must needs come upon Him. There was no mitigation of the awful judgment that sin deserved. The full flood-tide of judgment rolled over Him, and, as you see those waves and billows sweeping over Him – as you see Him going into the deep waters, and brought into the dust of death – you may say, 'That is my portion before God'. As a child of fallen Adam you could not be restored to innocence, or brought back in righteousness to God. Divine justice could only pass upon you the sentence of utter condemnation. If that condemnation had fallen upon you in your own person, you would have been lost forever, but, thank God! it has fallen upon you in the person of Him who took your place upon the cross. And when Christ hung upon that cross, God saw you there; and when He died and was buried you disappeared *judicially* as a child of Adam from God's sight for ever. God would have you to know this – it is a part of the gospel – "that our old man has been crucified with him", Romans 6:6.

It is on the ground of this great judicial act that the believer is entitled to reckon himself dead to sin, and alive to God in Christ Jesus, and when he is brought to this by the Spirit, he has deliverance. I think we may say that Adam is displaced by Christ

EXPERIMENTALLY,
when the believer gets deliverance.

All his efforts to improve himself are then at an end; and the awful misery of perpetual disappointment as to the success of those efforts is ended too, for he tastes the joy of being free from Adam, and is consciously in the liberty of life in Christ Jesus. This *experimental* setting aside of our old man is the proper and necessary counterpart of the *judicial* setting aside of which I have already spoken. When Paul said, "I am crucified with Christ: nevertheless, I live; yet not I, but Christ liveth in me" (Galatians 2:20), he expressed what he had really reached in the experience of his soul. He had done with himself. It was now for him, "Not I, but Christ". He not only believed that he had been set aside judicially before God at the cross, but he was in the good of a perfect deliverance for himself, so that not one thought of self-amendment crossed his mind. That is the grand test as to whether you have reached this. You might be very well up in the *doctrine* of deliverance, and yet all the time be secretly attempting to correct and improve yourself, and suffering a good deal of private vexation and disappointment on account of the failure of your attempts. I know how long I struggled on in this way myself, praying and striving to be more holy and Christ-like, and continually disappointed with the result. I do not think that it ever occurred to me in those days that I was trying to improve the man whom God had set aside. It was at a moment when I was utterly discouraged, and ready to give up the whole thing in complete despair, that God showed me how I was attempting to work upon the *old material* which He could only condemn, and that my disgust and despair as to myself were only a feeble echo of *His*. I shall never forget the joy of finding out that in the depth of my disgust with myself I was thoroughly at one with God. God had ceased to look for any good in *me*, and had Christ before Him, the perfect and infinitely acceptable Object of His heart; and I, in my nothingness, had ceased to look for good in myself, and was tasting the deep joy of being in Christ, and free to have Him as my Object; while, as to life, I entered in some degree into the blessedness of knowing that it was "not I, but Christ liveth in me".

Struggle and effort in themselves will never secure blessing, but by leading to despair and complete self-disgust they serve a divine purpose in the experience of the soul. I would rather see a soul in honest exercise, however legal he was, than see the light and careless acceptance of divine truth in the head without one atom of effect on the conscience or the heart. I do not think God gives us anything without preparing us for it by making us feel the need and the value of it. It is a divine principle that "He satisfieth *the longing soul*".

In these days, when ministry of the word is so plentiful and so accessible, and all difficulties in the way of learning truth intellectually are so minimized, it is of the deepest importance to remember that we only get *from God* what our souls have hungered and thirsted for. Soul-exercise will assuredly express itself in prayer, and the result will be deep and rich blessing. Do not rest until you are in the liberty of life in Christ Jesus! Remember that it is to set you consciously in this deliverance, and to maintain you in this liberty, that the Holy Spirit has taken up His abode in you, and these are the lines upon which He would set you and keep you.

Intimately connected with deliverance is the great fact that Adam is displaced

CHARACTERISTICALLY,
by Christ being formed in us.

The expression has just been under our notice – "Yet not I, but *Christ liveth in me*". Again, in chapter 4, the apostle says, "My little children, of whom I travail in birth again until *Christ be formed in you*". The great evil that the apostle had to contend with in Galatia was, that they were bringing in the law as an addition to Christ. Now what would be effected by the law, if all its precepts and regulations were carried out? It would form man in the flesh according to God; it would make *Adam* what he ought to be for God in this world; the law would form *Adam* in us. But the apostle indignantly repudiates this altogether. Peter and Barnabas might through fear dissemble, and keep up their religious character in the eyes of their legal brethren by not eating with the Gentiles, but Paul says, 'I have done with all that. The man whose appearance you are improving, and whose character you are maintaining by this parade of sanctity, I have done with. I, through the law, am dead to the law, that I might live unto God. I am crucified with Christ'. Who would think of doing anything to improve the appearance, or maintain the character, of a crucified man? That man had gone from God's eye and from Paul's eye too. Paul had entirely given up the man to whom law and ordinances applied.

Then, if that man was gone was there no other? Yes. Paul could not only speak of the setting aside of a man perfectly worthless, but of the bringing in of a MAN perfectly acceptable to God. "I live; yet not I, but Christ liveth in me". His great heart travailed in birth again for the Galatians that Christ might be formed in *them*. Religious ordinances could never effect this; it can only be effected as we go on in the Spirit. The Galatians had begun in the Spirit – they had begun by renouncing themselves and finding Christ to be everything – but they were now seeking to be made perfect by the flesh. A solemn picture of what our hearts are ever prone to do! The Spirit of God would maintain us constantly on the same line, for it is only as we keep upon the line where we found *deliverance* that we can stand fast in *liberty*. Upon that line we have done with ourselves as in the flesh; we have a new Person before us as the Object of faith and affection, and as we thus drop ourselves and have Christ as our Object, He is *formed in us*. What has been judicially accomplished at the cross has its counterpart by the Spirit in our souls, and it is upon that line that Christ is formed in us. We have before us a Man who has taken up on the cross our whole condition as in Adam, that He might end it in death; and now as the risen and glorified One, He fills, not only the heart of God, but the heart of everyone who is in the Spirit, with unspeakable rest and satisfaction.

It is thus that Christ is formed in us, and the effect of it is, that we come out in new character. The fruit of the Spirit – "love, joy, peace, long-suffering, gentleness, goodness, faith, meekness, temperance" – is what Christ is characteristically. It is not Adam elevated or improved, but Christ. In Colossians, this precious truth is further developed, where believers are said to have "put off the old man with his deeds; and have put on the new man, which is renewed in knowledge after the image of him that created him: where there is neither Greek nor Jew, circumcision nor uncircumcision, Barbarian, Scythian, bond nor free: but *Christ is all and in all*". On this ground we are exhorted to "put on therefore, as the elect of God, holy and beloved, bowels of mercies, kindness, humbleness of mind, meekness, long-suffering, forbearing one another, and forgiving one another, if any man have a quarrel against any: even as Christ forgave you, so also do ye. And above all these things put on love, which is the bond of perfectness". That is, Adam in every phase and form is set aside, Christ is everything and in all, and all that Christ is characteristically, takes the place of the selfish and hateful things characteristic of Adam. I am sure that the very mention of these things should have a deeply humbling effect upon us. I leave it to each one to ask his own heart how far all this has been effected and made good in him by the Spirit of God. But my purpose is not so much to ask how far you have got into this as to bring before you the blessed object at which God is aiming. If you understand the purpose of God, and the line upon which He is working, it will give character to your exercises and point to your prayers, and I am sure you will get on.

I can quite understand a young believer saying, 'All this is very beautiful, but where is the power to carry it out in a practical way?' The answer may be briefly given. *Our only power is the Spirit of God*, and Adam will only be displaced by Christ

PRACTICALLY,
as we walk in the Spirit.

You may learn from Romans 8:9 that the Spirit gives character to our state as Christians. We were once characterized by the presence of a nature that was nothing but sin: we are now characterized by the presence of the Holy Spirit. "Ye are not in the flesh, but in the Spirit, if so be that the Spirit of God dwell in you". The presence of a divine Person dwelling in us must bring in power, hence we read in Galatians 5:16, "This I say then, *walk in the Spirit*, and ye shall not fulfil the lust of the flesh". The Holy Spirit is dwelling in us to maintain us *practically* in the power of the truth that has been before us tonight. He would maintain us in perpetual distrust of ourselves, so that we should have no confidence in the flesh; He would maintain us in perpetual occupation with Christ, and give us unfailing joy in him. So long as we walk in the Spirit we do not fulfil the lust of the flesh.

If this is the case – if the Spirit of God is our only power – how important and solemn is that other word which we read in Ephesians 4:30, "*Grieve not the Holy Spirit of God*, whereby ye are sealed unto the day of redemption". If we grieve Him, we shall certainly not be supported by His power. And how may He be grieved? Surely by the allowance and toleration of that which He is here to resist; by making provision for the flesh to fulfil the lusts thereof; by attempting to cultivate and improve the man whom God has entirely set aside; by indifference to Christ. May God give everyone here to see the solemn importance of being on the line of the Spirit of God! If you are not on that line, you are failing to answer to the purpose of God in saving you, and you are sure to be disappointed in your expectations. On the other hand, if you are on the line, you will find that instead of Christianity being a failure and a disappointment, your heart will be filled with supreme satisfaction and joy, and you will be maintained here by the Spirit in a way that is pleasing to God.

Then there is a grand and crowning aspect of the subject before us which must not be forgotten. All the counsels of eternal love will have their full fruition in a coming day, when Adam will be superseded by Christ

## PHYSICALLY,
for we shall have bodies like His.

We have borne the image of the earthly, but we shall also bear the image of the heavenly. "Flesh and blood" – that order of bodily condition which pertains to Adam – "cannot inherit the kingdom of God". We shall have *spiritual bodies*; that is, bodies of which the vital principle will not be blood, but the Spirit of God. Christ – quickened by the Spirit and glorified at the right hand of God – is the First-fruits of the harvest, the First-born among *many brethren*, the Pattern, even as to bodily condition, of the heavenly company brought to God in grace on the ground of His death. He will change these bodies of humiliation into conformity to His body of glory; we shall be *like Him*, for we shall see Him as He is. Adam will be completely and eternally superseded by Christ.

I trust that you will prayerfully consider the great subject which I have thus imperfectly brought before you. I have said enough to show you how it is interwoven with the whole of Scripture, and how it touches every point of your spiritual life. The great question of all time – a question answered by the history of the ages, by the cross, and by the glory – a question to be answered now by our hearts – is, Which man will do for God – Adam or Christ? And when that is answered there arises another – Which man will do for me? Which man am I occupied with, or ministering to, or exhibiting? Adam or Christ?

———————

# DEVOTEDNESS

Song of Songs 2:1-4; Song of Songs 4:16.


I am sure that many of us have felt deeply the lack in our hearts of personal devotedness to Christ. We own with our lips, and I trust in our hearts, that the blessed Savior in glory is worthy that every bit of our being, from the heart's core to the finger-tips, should be for Him. I dare say many of us – I speak to those who, like myself, are young in the faith – have *longed*, and *prayed*, and *tried* to be more devoted to Christ; but our desires and efforts have not yielded a very satisfactory result. We have had to learn that we could not work up devotedness, or maintain it by resolution or effort.

Devotedness to Christ is an effect resulting from the operation of certain causes, and if these causes are operative in a divine way in our hearts, they will necessarily produce their proper effect. I wish to bring some of these causes before you, and I think a very important one is indicated in the opening verse of this chapter, where the Bride exclaims, "I am the rose of Sharon, and the lily of the valleys". She was so consciously assured of what she was in the eyes of the Bridegroom that she could take these precious words on her lips before Him. We cannot use such words as these if our hearts are not in the liberty of grace; if we do not know the wonderful place of favor that grace has conferred upon us, we cannot say, "I am the rose of Sharon, and the lily of the valleys".

It may be that there are some here tonight who have not got the assurance of pardon and everlasting security. You may be like an earnest and pious man of whose life I read lately, of whom his biographer says that near the end of his ministry, on one occasion, he said in public prayer, 'Oh, my God, I thank Thee I am within a hair-breadth of the full assurance of salvation'. The highest object of that dear man's heart was to be quite sure that he was saved. If this is *your* desire, I rejoice to tell you that God has removed every difficulty out of the way. You may have your sins pardoned, your soul saved, and divine assurance lodged in your heart forever. God has given His Savior-Son to go to the cross – the triumphant shout, "It is finished", has rung from His dying lips – God has raised Him from the dead and seated Him at His own right hand to be the glorious Witness to the value of His finished work, and Scripture is full of soul-assuring words for those who believe in Him. Here is one little verse for you. May God use it to give you *assurance* now! "To him give all the prophets witness, that through his name whosoever believeth in him shall receive remission of sins". Acts 10:43.

I want to confirm you as to *assurance*, but I earnestly long that everyone here should taste of the joys of acceptance, and be able to say, "I am the rose of Sharon, and the lily of the valleys". A great step on the way to devotedness is to know

WHAT YOU ARE IN CHRIST.

In connection with this let us read Ephesians 1:3 - 7. These verses bring before us the purpose and good pleasure of God's will to have a people before Him "holy and without blame", and not only that, but in all the acceptance of One who is "the Beloved" of His heart – a people who, through grace, can truly say, "I am the rose of Sharon, and the lily of the valleys". As soon as you take in this thought you will see that as a man in the flesh you are completely shut out, because no matter how earnest and zealous you were you never could bring yourself up to this. On the contrary, you find in yourself much that is unholy and hateful.

It may help us at this point if we read a few verses about two men and their experiences. Job 29:11 - 18; Job 40:3, 4; Job 42:5, 6; Philippians 3:4 - 6; Romans 7:18. We have here two specimen characters. No men could have a better moral and religious record than Job in the Old Testament and Saul of Tarsus in the New, but both these men were brought into the presence of God, and each one found that his best bit was corrupt. I should like you to notice the fact that it is not simply God's estimate of what these men were that is brought before us. It is *their own* estimate of themselves in God's presence. I believe many here accept as a truth that *God's* estimate of us is a very low one, but, beloved brethren, have we got in our souls what Job and Saul of Tarsus had in their souls? Job had this estimate of himself, "I am vile ... I abhor myself". Saul of Tarsus says, "I know that in me, that is, in my flesh, good does not dwell". I believe there are many who accept this in a certain way who have not experimentally learned it in their souls, and with the clearest knowledge of the doctrine they are not in the joy of divine acceptance because they have not done with themselves. They are looking to find some good in themselves, and in many cases without being conscious that they are doing so. Effort, disappointment, self-reproaches, and self-occupation, make up the weary round of their lives, with now and then, perhaps, a gleam of spiritual joy. No man's heart will ever be gladdened by the joy of divine acceptance – by the sunshine of favor that enables him to say, "I am the rose of Sharon, and the lily of the valleys" – until he has learned that there is not a single bit about him, as a man in the flesh, that does not deserve the judgment of God.

If you have learned that you are vile – if you abhor yourself – you will easily understand that if you are to be before God "holy and without blame" and in divine acceptance, it must be on the ground that you are in the acceptance of another Man. Now I ask, *Is there another man?* That is the very question, beloved young Christians, that the gospel answers. Yes, thank God, there is another Man. One who was once here and filled up the whole compass of man's responsibility with absolute perfection; One who has been to the cross to take up the whole question of sin and its consequences, and to maintain in connection therewith everything that was due to the glory of God; One who has died unto sin and done with it forever, but has been raised by the glory of the Father, and lives unto God as the accepted Man at His own right hand. He is there now "holy and without blame" before God, and in unclouded acceptance as "the Beloved". That is the Man God has had before His mind from eternity. Mark the word I have read in Ephesians 1, "Chosen ... in him before the foundation of the world". Consider the amazing fact that no created being, however exalted, would suffice to express God's thought as to man. A divine Person must become a man in order to furnish the man that was according to the thoughts of God's heart. As you think of Him in His life, death, and session in glory, are you not delighted to think of standing in the acceptance of THAT MAN? If we have learned with God that from the core to the circumference of our being there is not a sound spot in us, but that we are utterly under condemnation and death, it is blessed to find that the counsels of eternal love have purposed such an acceptance for us. So that now, through God's rich grace, knowing Christ as our Savior, we enter by the Holy Spirit into the joy of this new position, God has set us before Him in the acceptance and beauty of the One in whom He has found all His delight, and has given us His Spirit that we might be consciously in that acceptance.

You may ask, then, has God simply ignored our sinful state as children of Adam in giving us this wondrous acceptance? No, friend, that sinful state which has cost you so much exercise – which you have not been able to ignore – has been fully taken into account by God, and dealt with to His perfect satisfaction. It has been brought before Him at the cross, and has received its full and righteous condemnation there. "Our old man has been crucified with him". "For what the law could not do, in that it was weak through the flesh, God sending his own Son in the likeness of sinful flesh and for sin, condemned sin in the flesh", Romans 6:6; 8: 3.

It is thus in the liberty of grace and knowing what it is to be "accepted in the Beloved" that we can say, "I am the rose of Sharon, and the lily of the valleys". Are you consciously in that position? God would have our souls in the joy of this wonderful position; He would have us by His spirit free and happy in the joy of love that gives us such an acceptance. And this would carry us a great step on the way to devotedness to Christ.

But there is something else indicated in the second verse of our chapter, where we find the Bridegroom's reply, "As the lily among thorns, so is my love among the daughters". We have suggested in this verse, not so much what we are IN Christ, but

WHAT WE ARE TO CHRIST,

and I think the apprehension of this would touch our hearts even more than what has been already before us. There are a few words in John 13 that I should like to link with this. "Now before the feast of the Passover, when Jesus knew that his hour was come that he should depart out of this world unto the Father, having loved his own which were in the world, he loved them unto the end". I want my heart to nestle down more into the sweetness of those words – "his own" – "his own which were in the world". Not His own when He gets them home to the Father's house, made like Himself in glory, but His own *which are in the world*. By and by the lily will be taken to her destined place upon His breast in glory, but today she is among the thorns. We are in the world that had nothing but suffering, rejection, and death for our blessed Lord – it was a place of thorns for Him. He has gone away to the Father, but, if I may say so, He has left His heart behind Him. The blessed One who has entered into the rest and joy of the Father's presence has His treasure – the objects of His love – in this world, and we can neither express nor conceive the delight of His love even in such a company of "his own" as are here tonight. He can say of us now, in the joy of what we are to Him, "As the lily among thorns, so is my love among the daughters".

But, let us ask, how have we come to be "his own"? Ah! my brethren, to answer this we must go back and see ourselves in the hand of the Father's purpose before time began. "Thine they were", says the blessed Son, "and thou gavest them me". We were in the Father's purpose as a company worthy to be given to the Son as the expression of the Father's love to Him. Does not the thought of it bow our hearts in profound worship?

But another marvelous display of divine love was necessary before we could be "his own". "The good Shepherd giveth his life for the sheep". The purposes of sovereign love could only be carried out on the ground of redemption and the full maintenance of the divine glory in respect to sin, and to accomplish this the good Shepherd laid down His life for the sheep. I am sure we have often lingered with delight over the tenth chapter of John, and many a weary sinner's heart has been cheered by the grace of such words as, "I give unto then eternal life; and they shall never perish, neither shall any pluck them out of my hand". But assurance *for us* of eternal security is not the principal or most precious thought in this and the succeeding verse. It is rather the delight of the Shepherd in securing "his own" for Himself. For this He died and for this He still acts in power and love, that He may never lose that which cost Him so much to win. The Father, too, acts in divine power, and love to the same end. Precious unity, in the Father and the Son, of purpose and delight as to us! How differently we should carry ourselves in the world if our hearts knew more of this!

Let me call your attention for a moment to this matchless scene in John 13. Jesus was leaving the world and going to the Father, and it was *with this in view* that He rose from supper, took a towel and girded Himself, and began to wash the disciples' feet. Peter, for our benefit, objected, and then the key to the Lord's action was furnished by the words, "If I wash thee not, thou hast no part with Me". He who was going to the Father – into the untold blessedness and joy of *the Father's world* – would have "his own" to have part with Him. The very best thing that the deep love of His heart could think of for us is that we should have part with Him in that wonderful circle with the Father. To this end He serves in active love with a view to remove every spot and stain that would unfit us for part with Him. His love declares that He must have every spot removed that would hinder you from enjoying along with Him His portion with the Father. How far you and I have been in a condition to get the good of that service is another matter. If you ask me to explain what part with Him is, I cannot tell you. When I think of it, I feel like a little child looking out upon an immeasurable ocean of blessedness and joy. I long that your heart and mine should be more awake to the reality of it all, and that we may allow our hearts to sink down into the depths of love that would give us nothing less than this, because of what we are *to Him* – love that can say of us, "As the lily among thorns, so is my love among the daughters".

There is a very practical and experimental side to this which is brought before us in Philippians 2:12 - 17. When our blessed Lord was here He was truly as a one "among thorns", and now that He is gone the same mind and character are to be found in "his own". Salvation, in this experimental sense, is nothing less than the complete displacement of our own will. The willing and the doing of God's pleasure being wrought in us, and we ourselves working it out with fear and trembling, we are found in this world in a totally new character. Doing all things without murmuring and disputing, and being blameless and harmless, the sons of God without rebuke, in the midst of a crooked and perverse nation, among whom we shine as lights in the world, we should be found practically and experimentally "as the lily among thorns". The Lord grant that this may be so increasingly for His Name's sake!

The knowledge of what we are *in* Christ and

*to* Him prepares our hearts for what I may call the third step on the way to devotedness. It has been said that the end of all God's ways with us is to make

CHRIST EVERYTHING TO US,

and the next verse of our chapter is the language of a heart that has reached this. "As the apple tree among the trees of the wood, so is my beloved among the sons. I sat down under his shadow with great delight, and his fruit was sweet to my taste. He brought me to the banqueting house, and his banner over me was love". His deep perfections are the Same yesterday, and today, and forever. The Bride in chapter 5 seeks to enumerate His excellencies, but she has to stop short and say, "Yea, he is altogether lovely". What an Object for your heart and mine! One of whom every thought might well yield, "unchanging, fresh delight!" If we have learned what we are *in* Him and *to* Him, it is surely that our hearts may be free to enter with absorbing delight and satisfaction into what He is in Himself. We are thus delivered from ourselves not only by learning our own worthlessness, but by the positive power of a new Object. Notice the striking contrast between the empty and thirsty man in Psalm 42, occupied with his soul and its needs, and the full and overflowing man of Psalm 45, whose heart is absorbed by the King in His beauty! It is just like the transition from "If any man thirst", to the overflowing satisfaction of "Let him come unto ME, and drink, He that believeth on ME, as the scripture hath said, out of his belly shall flow rivers of living water", John 7:37, 38.

Beloved young Christian, is that living Person now in heavenly glory really the Object of your heart? For some time after I knew the Savior I used to think of Him as One who had lived and died on earth long years ago, and I well remember the day when I knelt down with a dear brother who prayed that we might know Christ as a living Person in heavenly glory, and it dawned upon me that there was a present Object for my heart in heaven. Your heart will never be satisfied until that glorified Christ becomes its Object bright and fair.

Then, having such a Person as the object of your heart, you will sit down under His shadow with great delight and find His fruit sweet to your taste. Mark the words, "under his shadow". I see many Christians today suffering from spiritual sunstroke. The sun was made "to rule the day", and is a figure of the influences of the day. Christians who are constantly exposed to the influences that are around us in this world know that these things have a tendency to dry us up and paralyze us spiritually. I am sure some of you know what a blessed restorative of spiritual vigor it is after a long active day of business life to get away from contact with men and things, and to sit down "under his shadow". Isaiah 32 speaks of Him as "the shadow of a great rock in a weary land". I dare say some of you know what it is to be travelers in a "weary land". Personal sorrows and difficulties, family or business cares, and perhaps worldly temptations or persecutions crowd in upon you; and your spiritual freshness is not quite what it used to be. You need to sit down under His shadow, and the way is open for you to go to that sweet retreat and find there how He refreshes your soul.

Then there is not only shelter but abiding satisfaction to be found in thus sitting under His shadow. "His fruit was sweet to my taste". All the present grace of His heart, and all the activity and outcome of that grace, and all the deep perfections of His adorable Person, become the food and satisfaction of our souls. It is there, too, that we learn His mind and pleasure, and acquire a sense of what is suited to Him. We must know what it is to *sit down* before we *stand up* and *run forth* to serve. It is impossible to overestimate the importance of this training for service. Mary of Bethany is an example of this, familiar to everyone. She "sat at Jesus' feet, and heard his word", and thus was she prepared for the most precious service that ever was rendered to Him.

Beloved young Christians, are you in the secret personal history of your own souls tasting the joy of sitting down under His shadow? Are you finding continual satisfaction in Himself? If so, you will not want religious novels or worldly entertainments – you will not be found going in for things on the ground that there is no harm in them – you will not be in any way dependent for happiness on the sin-stained streams of earth. Five minutes under His shadow affords more real delight than a lifetime of the pleasures of the earth or of the world. How differently we shall estimate our lives when we look back over them from the judgment seat of Christ! How we shall judge as supreme folly the way in which we have allowed our hearts to be carried off by little things that were not worth a thought – the way in which we have allowed the devil to deceive us and occupy us with earthly things (cares as well as pleasures) when we might have had a portion like this. May the Lord draw our hearts more after Himself!

There is one more lovely touch which must not be passed over, expressed in the words, "He brought me to the banqueting house, and his banner over me was love". The banqueting house was the place of royal pleasure – the place where the king had his own delights – and it was in that place that his love was known by the bride. Is there anything that answers to it now? I believe there is. If Christ has made Himself everything to you, you will want to find the place where He has set His name, and where His own assemble to remember Him, and where they can have the joy of His presence, according to John 14:18. There is such a thing upon this earth today as being gathered together *to His name*, and, when so gathered, having His company. His first activity in resurrection was to gather together His own. To this end He satisfied the sorrowing heart of Mary Magdalene, He relieved the soiled conscience of Peter, and He recovered the straying feet of the two who had gone to Emmaüs. He wanted a company where His love could have its own free course, and make its inexpressible riches known; where the Father's name could be declared to His brethren in the new position and relationship into which He had brought them on the ground of His death; and where He could make their hearts glad with His own joy. Can you say that the Lord has brought you to such a place – even to His own banqueting house and beneath the banner of His love?

The knowledge of what the assembly is to Christ is necessary in order to get a proper conception of His love. As an individual I may say "the Son of God, who loved me", but I do not really apprehend the love of Christ unless I think of the whole church. "Christ also loved the Church, and gave himself for it". It is a wonderful thing to say, but there is *an adequate object* for the love of Christ, and that object is the church. The more you enter into this, the more you will love your brethren, the more you will understand the Lord's pleasure in having His own around Himself, and the more also you will long to be found so gathered as to be able to say, "He brought me to the banqueting house, and his banner over me was love".

You may think that I am a long time in coming to the subject of

DEVOTEDNESS TO CHRIST,

but my object was to occupy you with the causes that produce it rather than with the result itself. If these causes are divinely operative the effect is certain. If these things really get into your soul they will lead to a result which is indicated in chapter 4: 16.

"Let my beloved come into his garden, and eat his pleasant fruits".

In chapter 2 we are learning what He is *for us* – we are feeding upon *His fruit* – but in the verse I have just read we are entirely for Him. The Bride invites Him to come into *His garden* and to eat *His pleasant fruits*. She is exclusively, and entirely, for Him, and that is devotedness. There is neither effort nor bondage about it; it is the happy and spontaneous *effect* that flows from the operation of the *motive causes* which we have been considering. We read it in New Testament language in such words as these, "The love of Christ constraineth us; because we thus judge, that if one died for all, then were all dead: and that he died for all, that they which live should not henceforth live unto themselves, but unto Him which died for them, and rose again", 2 Corinthians 5:14, 15. Now, beloved are we living unto Him? Do our lives in some small degree bear the impress of true devotedness? You may say as it has often been said, that this is all very well for people who have nothing to do but to go about preaching, but that the trials and difficulties of practical, everyday life render it impossible for most Christians. This is a great mistake. To begin with, the only thing which a Christian has to do in this world – whether he breaks stones on the road-side or preaches to thousands – is to live unto Christ. Then the trials and difficulties, which so many complain of, are intended for the very purpose of *helping* and not *hindering* devotedness to Christ.

Read the first half of the verse which we are now considering. "Awake, O north wind; and come, thou south; blow upon my garden, that the spices thereof may flow out". If we are going on with God, both the north wind of adversity and the south wind of prosperity will bring out fruit for Christ. I have seen believers who never got on well until the north wind blew on them. It was in the hour of family affliction, or business trial, or personal suffering, that their souls brightened up in a wonderful way. You have never had any trials or difficulties to compare with Paul's. He lost his means, his reputation, his liberty, and the fellowship of his brethren; he knew what it was to be an old, forsaken, hungry prisoner; and yet what does he say about it all? "I know that this shall turn to my salvation through your prayer, and the supply of the Spirit of Jesus Christ, according to my earnest expectation and my hope, that in nothing I shall be ashamed, but that with all boldness, as always, so now also Christ shall be magnified in my body, whether it be by life, or by death", Philippians 1:19, 20.

The cold, keen blast of the north wind was sweeping over him, but it was only serving to bring out the precious fruit in the garden of the Beloved.

It is when the south wind blows that we are most severely tested as to whether we are really for Christ. When our circumstances and surroundings are easy and comfortable there is a strong tendency to settle down and go to sleep. No one needs so much grace as the man who is surrounded by means to make himself happy in this world. It is a wonderful sight to see a Christian surrounded with everything that would naturally tempt him to settle down here, with his heart kept true to Christ. I do not know any fruit more precious to the Lord than that. When a man has every opportunity of living unto himself, and yet, through grace, is devoted to Christ, there is a rich outflow of the spices that are so fragrant to the heart of the Beloved.

When Mary of Bethany broke her alabaster box and poured its rich treasure on the feet of Jesus and wiped His feet with her hair, it was a picture of true devotedness. Her *all* and *herself* were FOR HIM. There is a beautiful fitness in the fact that we never hear of her again. She had expended herself on Him. Martha could no doubt say, "My beloved is mine"; but Mary had tasted the deeper joy of confessing, "I am my beloved's" It is one thing to say, Christ for me, and another to say, Me for Christ. The latter is true devotedness. Who can tell what Mary's act was to the Father and the Son? So precious was it to the Lord that He has ordained that wherever *His devotedness* is spoken of mention must be made of *hers*. That ointment is never to cease yielding its fragrance, wheresoever the gospel is preached.

Of similar character was the noble act of David's men, who heard their master long for water of the well of Bethlehem, and who broke through the enemies' host in jeopardy of their lives to satisfy his desire. The issue of their service was not very great in the eyes of men. Perhaps few knew anything about it, and probably it was criticized as a foolhardy adventure. But that cruse of water poured out upon the ground was expressive of lives poured out in devotion to the Lord's Anointed; it showed that those mighty men were devoted to David, and it secured for them a wonderful place in the day of his power and kingdom.

Our place in the coming kingdom-glory will be determined by the measure of our fidelity and devotedness to Christ in His present rejection. May the motive causes, which we have been considering, be so powerfully operative in our hearts by the Holy Spirit, that they may result in our being here more distinctly and devotedly FOR CHRIST, and thus may our "Beloved come into his garden, and eat his pleasant fruits".

———————

# "DAILY"

There are many here tonight who are young in the faith; they have not long taken upon their lips the confession of the Lord Jesus. I speak with an earnest desire to help and encourage such, and I should like to bring before you six things that will have a place in your everyday life if you go on with God. The first of them is brought before us in Acts 17:10 - 12.

## DAILY SEARCHING OF THE SCRIPTURES

It is of great importance to the welfare of your soul that you should have, and cultivate, an appetite for the Holy Scriptures. But everything depends upon the spirit and attitude in which we approach the Scriptures. It is possible to study the Bible in schoolboy fashion, and to learn divinity just as people learn geology or botany. I do not want to encourage you to do that; there is already too much of it. We are not only told that the Bereans "searched the scriptures", but we are told *why* they searched. They heard the preaching of Paul and Silas, and "*received the word with all readiness of mind, and searched the scriptures daily, whether those things were so*". Wonderful things were brought to their ears, and they were not skeptical or indifferent, they "received the word with all readiness of mind", and they searched the Scriptures because they had received the word of the apostles. They searched, not like the antiquary who pores over an old will with curiosity or scientific interest, but like the person who has been told, and who has received the report, that a great legacy is bequeathed to him in it. I thank God that many of you have received the report of the marvelous blessings of His grace, but I fear that some of you have not been sufficiently interested in them to search the Scriptures daily, whether these things are so. The result is that you are not so stable as you ought to be; and if you were challenged as to some of the blessings which you think you have received; you might not be able to give a very good "reason of the hope that is in you".

There is often a carelessness amongst the children of God as to divine things which has no parallel in the ordinary affairs of life. If a man buys an estate, he does not content himself with the bare word of the vendor; he will have the deeds searched with the utmost care to be quite sure the title is good. If a man has property left him in America, and a detailed account of it is sent to him, you may be sure that he will read it carefully through, and that more than once. If I were to go to some wealthy merchant and tell him that the King had conferred upon him the honor of knighthood, he would insist on seeing the official documents which would verify the statement. The more important a thing is, the more anxious people are to be sure about it, and I think if we got a right sense of the immensity of the very smallest bit of Christian blessing, we should go to the Scriptures as the Bereans did to make quite sure that these things were so. I think where there is carelessness as to this, it indicates that we have not a right sense in our hearts of the greatness of Christian blessings, or they would become matters of more earnest and anxious inquiry. These things are so important – the issues at stake are so vital – that we should take nothing on trust, even if the speaker be an apostle.

I am often surprised that Christians who have listened for years – apparently with interest and attention – to the ministry of the word know so little of divine things. They seem to enjoy the ministry, their faces are bright in the meetings, and yet when you come to talk to them you find that very little of it has got into their souls. I believe the secret is that they listen to what is said, but value it so little that they do not take the trouble of going to the Scriptures to verify it for themselves. Ministry has its own blessed and important place, but I do not believe that any ministry will be of permanent profit to our souls if it is not followed by searching of the scriptures.

Timothy, Paul's child in the faith, was exhorted by the apostle to "give attendance to reading", and to "meditate upon these things; give thyself wholly to them, that thy profiting may appear to all", 1 Timothy 4:13 - 15. Further, as a *servant* he was to be a "workman that needeth not to be ashamed, rightly dividing the word of truth"; and as a *man of God* he was to know that "all scripture is given by inspiration of God, and is profitable for doctrine, for reproof, for correction, for instruction in righteousness; that the man of God may be perfect, thoroughly furnished unto all good works", 2 Timothy 2:15; 3: 16, 17. In connection with this there is an exhortation in 2 Timothy 1:13, to which we might do well to take heed – "Hold fast the form of sound words", or as a new translation gives it – "Have an outline of sound words". Timothy was to have in his mind an outline of the truth so that it was clear before him. When I was at school, we had sometimes to draw outline maps from memory, and very strange outlines used to be presented, that would have puzzled anyone to tell what country they were intended to be like. Now suppose someone asked you to give an outline of the truth of Christianity, could you do it? It is the will of God that we should have a clear outline of the truth before our minds, and we cannot have this without searching the Scriptures. Otherwise, our thoughts on divine things will be vague and indefinite, and we may become the prey of some plausible system of error, of which there are such endless varieties at the present day. If we desire to be tenacious of the truth, it is more than ever necessary that we should search the Scriptures "daily".

Searching gives the idea of a definite object being in view. A great deal of Bible reading is profitless because aimless. The reader is seeking for nothing and finds it. I believe that we profit most when our souls are interested in certain subjects, and exercised before the Lord about them, and we turn to the Scriptures to search whether these things are so. There are surely many things with each one of us that we are more or less anxious to have divine light upon. Many of us do not know the *doctrines* of Scripture very clearly: questions arise as to *practical details* in our walk: surely each one of us has exercise as to our *soul-experiences;* and all these things should constrain us to "search the scriptures".

And remember it must be daily! I press upon every young Christian here the necessity for the *daily* study of the Scriptures. You cannot maintain a vacuum in your mind; if it is not occupied with divine things it will be with human or earthly things. The habit of searching the Scriptures grows upon you as you go on with it, but if you neglect it you soon lose a relish for it. I have heard Christians say something like this – 'I wish I could enjoy the word of God more. When I read my Bible, I don't get the blessing that some people do. I hear So-and-so say how his soul is refreshed by the word, but I don't get it'. I like to ask such persons, How often do you read the Bible? Once a week? Or once a month? The one who reads his Bible most is the one who enjoys it most, and who turns to it with the greatest delight. On the other hand, if you neglect the Bible today you will have less taste for it tomorrow, still less the day after, and so on until it becomes a dry book to you. You must make a point of it that you are in company with the Scriptures *every* day. It is not a question of a great deal – you perhaps have not time for that – but you must have it daily.

2. "Blessed is the man that heareth me, watching daily at my gates, waiting at the posts of my doors. For whoso findeth me findeth life, and shall obtain favor of the

Lord", Proverbs 8:34, 35.

You will get very little blessing for your soul, and you will make no spiritual progress, even by daily searching of the Scriptures, unless you are also

## DAILY WATCHING AT WISDOM'S GATES

The great central Figure of Scripture must be the Object of your affections, or you will read to little profit. In short, Christ must be before your heart, or you will miss the kernel of every truth in Scripture. The allusion in these verses is to an Eastern court, where certain favored ones are admitted to the privilege of being near the monarch. In the first of Esther, we read of seven princes who "saw the king's face". Others may read his commands and hear about him at a distance, but these stand in his presence and hear his voice. Are you going in for this, beloved young Christians? The glorious Person who gave full delight to the heart of God has set His love upon us! He has revealed Himself to us as the One who has found His delight in us. Is that Person so holding your heart – are you so delighting in Him – that your whole inner life consists in hearing Him, in watching *daily* at His gates, and waiting at the posts of His doors? The grand secret of spiritual freshness and soul-prosperity is to have Christ so before the heart that we are attracted to *Himself*, with intense longing to know Him better. Now, beloved, let us challenge our hearts as to this! Are we on the alert to improve our acquaintance with Christ? The great defect of modern Christianity is that there is so little affection for Christ. Many hear what is called a clear gospel, and trusting the Person and work of Christ they get the assurance of the Scriptures that they will never perish, and this seems to satisfy them and they settle down upon it and go to sleep. There is not the earnest longing after Himself – the *watching daily* at His gates. Did it ever occur to you that Christ values your affections? You belong to Him; you are the object of His love; you are "His own". Your heart is Christ's property: is it His dwelling-place? His love counts on your giving Him a place in your affections, so that He may dwell in your heart "by faith". If He does dwell there, you may depend upon it that you will be watching daily at His gates – not only seeking His benefits, but longing after *Himself*, and finding it the deepest joy of your heart that you are admitted to personal acquaintance with Him.

Look at Mary of Magdala – in her day a lovely example of this precious affection for Christ! *Apostles* did not attract her heart; she let them go to their homes without her. *Angels* – the highest order in creation – speak to her, but leave her unsatisfied. She does not even turn to look properly at *the supposed gardener*. She has forgotten *herself* – a weak, and defenseless woman – as she says, "Sir, if thou hast borne him hence, tell me where thou hast laid him, and I will take him away". It was *Himself* that her devoted heart longed after with all the intensity of its affection. She watched at His gates and waited at the posts of His doors; and did she not "obtain favor of the Lord"? No such message of divine love as that which she carried was ever entrusted to human lips before.

Andrew and John knew something of what I am speaking of, when the longing of their hearts was expressed in the question – "Rabbi, where dwellest thou?" John 1:38, 39. They wanted to be in His company; they were in their day found watching at His gates and waiting at the posts of His doors. And what favor they obtained! "He saith unto them, Come and see. They came and saw where he dwelt, and abode with him that day". Was it not a royal day for them? Do you think they will ever forget it? it is a glorious day for the heart when it makes *personal acquaintance* with Christ. I dare say there are some here tonight who could tell you that the deep joy of that hour was infinitely greater than the joy of the hour when they learned the perfect efficacy of His work. Nor would the Lord have this to be a transient experience. They "abode with him that day" – a day typical of the whole present period – and though He is no longer in the world He would have us abiding with Him. His love could think of no sweeter portion for us than to have a *part with Him,* and no service of His love is more precious to a devoted heart than that washing by which He removes the defilement of the world from our feet, that we may have a *part with Himself* where He dwells with the Father (John 13). Does not your heart long to taste more deeply the blessedness of the one who watches daily at His gates, and waits at the posts of His doors?

Paul is another example of this when he tells us that he counted all things but loss, for the excellency of the knowledge of Christ Jesus his Lord, and that he counted all things but dung that he might win Christ to know him. To attain this, he was pressing on as a man wholly absorbed by one object. To use once more the words before us, he was watching daily at His gates, and waiting at the posts of His doors. And did he not "obtain favor of the Lord"? Was it a small thing to be able to say as an experimental reality, "our citizenship is in heaven"? or to say, "I have learned, in whatsoever state I am, to be satisfied in myself"? or to say, "I can do all things, through Christ which strengtheneth me"? He did indeed verify the blessing spoken of in Proverbs 8:34, 35. May our hearts be very much drawn after that blessed Person in glory, that we may verify it too!

3. "I cry unto thee daily", Psalm 86:3. I wish to remind you of the great importance of

## DAILY PRAYER

and I purposely left the subject of prayer until I had said a little about the affections of the heart being after Christ, because nothing will be more changed than your prayers if you are really after Christ. If Christ is before our hearts, we feel the hindrances and the difficulties, and we understand the need for prayer in a very different way from one who has not Christ as his object. There never was upon the earth a man who was so continually in the spirit of prayer as the blessed Lord, for there never was one whose heart was so devoted to God. It was the very excellence of His devotedness to God that made Him so entirely dependent – that made Him so pre-eminently the Man of prayer. The more our hearts are set upon Christ in glory, the more we are devoted to His interests here, and the more do we feel our weakness and dependence. We feel that everything here is against us; we are conscious of the opposition around and within, and we become more and more *men of prayer.* I think you will allow that the apostle excelled all other saints in devotedness to Christ, and there never was one so saturated with the spirit of prayer. I am sure of this, that if our hearts are set upon Christ in glory the effect will be that we shall be much on our knees.

Allow me to give you a few practical words as to your prayers. Keep clear of the unprofitable habit of merely saying your prayers. Christendom is full of solemn warnings as to the tendency of our hearts to drop into a routine of religious forms. It is a very great loss to the soul, to get into the habit of repeating substantially the same words in prayer every day. It is not real prayer at all. We read – *"In everything* by prayer and supplication with thanksgiving, let your requests be made known unto God". Philippians 4:6. How can you do that if you are using the same form of words day after day, and week after week? Today is not like yesterday, and tomorrow will not be like today. If you are really with God you will be sensitive to the fresh needs of every day. God delights to have our confidence as to every need and care. Then let us cultivate a child's confidence, and a child's simplicity as we come to Him in prayer. Bring the trying circumstances of today, and the expected difficulties and perplexities of tomorrow, to the blessed God who tells you to cast all your care upon Him, for He cares for you. Be simple: give up the long preface: do not feel it necessary to quote a dozen scriptures: ask as a needy and confiding child would ask its parent. If I might venture to say one word about the *prayer meeting* it would be this: I do not believe any brother should take part unless he has some definite petition to present. I have been in prayer meetings where I have felt as if brothers began without knowing a single thing they were going to ask for, and discoursed about every subject that happened to come into their minds. This may be profitable religious excrcise, but it is certainly not *prayer.*

Then if we are really set for Christ, as I said before, we realize our dependence in a deeper way, because our faith connects the glory of *His name* with everything in our daily life, and we become sensible that it is only as we are maintained by divine power that we can be for Him here. Such a one has many an exercise that others miss who are less devoted, but he enjoys oftentimes the deep blessedness of communion with God, while they are living and walking "as men". The more your heart is set for Christ, the more you will be characterized by humility and dependence, which will find their expression in *daily prayer*.

4. "Give us this day our daily bread". Matthew 6:11. I suppose that we all believe the

## DAILY BREAD

here referred to is that which meets the need of the body. Those who know not God seek after what they may eat and drink, and what they may put on. Their concern is all about the body; we can rejoice that our Father knows we have need of these things, and *He cares* for us in every detail of that need. But I wish to use these words tonight to impress upon you the importance of having your *soul nourished* every day. We need food convenient for our bodies every day, and it is not less needful to have something fresh from the Lord for our souls. Now, come, what have you had from the Lord today? 'I have been reading a very good book, and part of one of the periodicals'. I am glad to hear it, but did you get anything from the Lord? 'I have read one or two chapters in the Bible'. I am very thankful for that, but still you might read many chapters without getting anything from the Lord to meet the present need of your soul. Reading and hearing are like looking at the food, but it is another thing to get the good of it. Food is that which satisfies a craving – a felt need – and unless we have an appetite there is not even the desire for it. It is one of the great principles of God's ways that He "satisfieth the *longing* soul", and fills "the *hungry* with good things". Hence the subject of the soul's *daily bread* is a deeply experimental one. The food of which I speak is the gracious supply to our souls of that which answers the exercises, and meets the need of which we become conscious in our experience day by day. I do not mean your *external* need, but the need of your heart and spirit, in the various experiences of your soul.

One or two scripture illustrations may perhaps serve to make my meaning clear. On the night of the Passover in Egypt the children of Israel had – as we often hear – the blood of the lamb to make them *safe* and the word of Jehovah to make them *sure*: but they had also the lamb roast with fire for their *food*. The soul in the position thus typified has a perfect shelter from judgment in the precious blood of Christ, and a perfect assurance in the word of God, but has he no longings, no exercises, *no experience?* He has escaped the judgment, it is true, but he feels how near it has been to him; he is conscious how truly he deserved it. It is a solemn hour for him; he has no doubt as to his safety, but still, it is a solemn hour, for God in His holiness is passing over. Is there no food for him? Is there no gracious supply of the very thing which will meet his present need? Indeed, there is: he feeds with self-judgment ("with bitter herbs they shall eat it") on the Lamb "roast with fire". He appropriates to himself, and takes into his moral being, the precious fact that Christ has fully borne the judgment of God, and this meets the hunger of his soul. He loves to think of the spotless perfection of the Victim, of the love that made Him willing to bear the judgment, and of the infinite value of that divine work which has exhausted forever the judgment under which he lay. The meaning of Calvary's darkness, of the cry of the Forsaken One, of the triumph shout, "It is finished", becomes great and real. The soul enters into it, takes possession of it by faith, *feeds upon it.* I trust we all know something of this!

At another stage of their experience the children of Israel were found in the wilderness – the place of no human resources – but they had *food* there, and they had it *every day.* Those who have seen the salvation of God, and have escaped from the judgment-land by faith in the death and resurrection of Christ, find themselves in the wilderness; that is, in a place where they have fresh needs and exercises every day, without any human resources to satisfy those needs or answer those exercises. Alas, the perverseness and rebellion of Israel only too well represent our own. How often have our hearts refused the lessons of the wilderness, and sought to find a more pleasant and easy path where *daily* exercises of soul might be avoided!

In Egypt we had no such exercises, and to escape them have we not often been ready to make a captain of our own choice and go back to be sustained by human resources? How truly is the wilderness the place where we learn what is in our heart! Deuteronomy 8:2.

But the manna fell *every day.* If they had *fresh hunger* every day they had also fresh *food* every day. And, beloved brethren, for the renewed needs and exercises of every day we may have renewed supplies of heavenly grace to sustain us in the path of faith. There is One in glory who knows every bit of the wilderness, for He has been through it. He is out of it now, but from where He is in glory, we may have the daily supply of grace suited to our wilderness experiences, from One who knows well what wilderness circumstances are. Paul would have liked to escape from the exercise caused by the thorn for the flesh (2 Corinthians 12), but he was better off with it than without it, for along with it he got what I think answers to the manna – "My grace is sufficient for thee". I am sure if you have known anything at all of this you will say that it is infinitely better to have *the exercise and the grace* than to be without them. As I said, this is very experimental, and when we come to experimental things we find out where we are. *Doctrines* will not help you in your everyday needs and exercises; you must have the supply that is suited to them fresh from heaven. You must have *daily bread*. The manna that sustained you through yesterday's experience will not do for today. You must have fresh grace from the Lord in glory for every hour of need. Thus the heart's intercourse with heaven is kept up from day to day, and our affections become more and more attracted to the Person and the place from whence our supplies come.

We have all, I trust, passed through some stages of divine experience. We have been – through grace – awakened, converted, led to trust in Jesus, and brought into peace with God on the ground of Christ's death and resurrection, but at this point many seem to stop. They have got all they want and they settle down and go to sleep – that is, they live more or less on the same principles as unconverted men. I ask you, young believer, whether it would not make a great difference in your life, if you were to accept a path where human resources cannot sustain you, and where you have to look continually to the Lord in glory for the supply of *daily grace* to carry you on. You cannot get on, as a Christian, on your own resources. Your only strength lies in "the grace that is in Christ Jesus", and you may have it fresh as the food of your soul every day and hour. This would keep us out of all ruts and formalities – there would be nothing humdrum or mechanical about our lives – because every day would bring fresh experiences of the grace of Christ, and the sense of His interest in us would knit our hearts more and more to Himself. May the Lord preserve us from becoming insensible to our daily need, or indifferent to the *present grace* that His love delights to supply as our *daily bread.*

5. "If any man will come after me, let him deny himself, and take up his cross daily, and follow me", Luke 9:23.

I am quite sure that you would shrink from the

DAILY CROSS

if you did not know something of the grace of which I have been speaking. It is feeding on the *daily bread* that enables us to sustain the *daily cross,* just as in Luke 14 you get the Supper first and then the building and the fighting. How could you build or fight unless you were first fed? In a similar way in Hebrews 13:10 you are first fed from the altar and then (verse 13) you are called to make a journey. When God was going to send Elijah a long journey, He fed him first. 1 Kings 19. You must feed upon the heavenly grace that comes from Christ, or you will never have the heart to "go forth unto him". It is when you have learned that all your supplies come *from* Him that you are willing to go forth *to* Him in the place of shame and reproach, which answers to the daily cross of Luke 9. You take up a path that exposes you to shame and contempt every day. If a man was seen bearing his cross everybody knew that he had done with the world, and as long as he remained in it he was an object of reproach. To bear the cross is to accept the reproach of being connected with that which is mean and despicable in the eyes of men. A crucified man was inconceivably despicable to both the Jew and the Greek, and we must not forget that though the cross is so highly honored now in name, it is not really one whit more acceptable to men; and if we are true to the Man who died on the cross we shall be targets for the taunts and the scorn of the world. The *daily cross* is not bodily affliction or the ordinary trials of life, as so many suppose, for these things are not peculiar to Christians, they are the common lot of mankind. The daily cross is the acceptance day by day of a path and a portion which, so far as this world goes, is one of dishonor and reproach.

You may depend upon it that it will never be easy to the flesh to follow Christ and to bear His reproach. How much we need to remember those words of the Holy Spirit – "Forasmuch then as Christ hath suffered for us in the flesh, *arm yourselves likewise with the same mind:* for he that hath suffered in the flesh hath ceased from sin!" 1 Peter 41. If we are true to Christ it will involve the surrender of much that we naturally esteem – the praise of men, and the honors of life in this world. When our eye gets off Christ, we shirk the cross, and try to avoid the scorn and the sneers of the world. It is a long time since I read *Pilgrim's Progress,* but I have not forgotten that *Shame* was one of the worst enemies he met with. A great soul-winner said that it cost him a struggle to give away a tract; and you may be sure that every bit of real testimony for Christ will cost you something. If you are acting in the flesh of course you will escape this, for *he* is not ashamed of his doings, and you may be very well pleased with yourself and your service. But true testimony involves the denial of self, and the daily cross, for discipleship will never be a path of liberty to the flesh. As you keep your eye upon Christ you do not seek to gratify the flesh but to walk in the Spirit, and you are able to sing from your heart:

*"Savior, I long to follow Thee,*
*Daily the cross to bear".*

The child of God walking in the Spirit does not dread the cross, he longs for it. Like Moses, he esteems the reproach of Christ greater riches than the treasures in Egypt, for he has respect unto the recompense of the reward. As you take up the daily cross you will have a present reward in the sense of the Lord's approval; and by and by it will be your immeasurable gain in the thousand years of kingdom glory, and your joy forever. May the Lord encourage all our hearts in this matter!

6. "Exhort [encourage] one another daily", Hebrews 3:13.

There is immense need for such an exhortation as this, for there is a constant tendency in our hearts to be "discouraged because of the way". The young especially need

DAILY ENCOURAGEMENT,

and it is a great privilege from the Lord to be

able to "encourage one another". I am afraid that many souls backslide and drift away simply because we are not near enough to the Lord, and have not sufficient affection to give them a word of encouragement. It is no use trying to set the old man down; you may lecture and hammer at him with all your might, but he can stand all the blows that you give him. You must keep your eye on that which is of God in the saints, and lay yourself out to encourage that. There is no other way to help one another. There is something which is of God in every saint; it may be very weak and small, but we must build on that – we must encourage that. You will see what I mean in the epistles. Take the Galatians; they were in an awful state, in danger of leaving the very foundations of Christianity, and yet Paul says, "I have confidence in you through the Lord, that ye will be none otherwise minded", Galatians 5:10. We have to look at the saints from a divine stand-point, and we shall then recognize, as Balaam did, what they are in God's thoughts and purposes, and we shall count upon His Spirit's work in them, in spite of much that would turn our hearts from them if we judged after the sight of our eyes and the hearing of our ears. We must count on the work of God in the souls of His saints, and seek to help and encourage that which is of Himself in every way. As the Spirit's work in the soul prospers, Christ supersedes and displaces the flesh and the world, and this is the way of true sanctification.

Let none of us think that this is only for teachers and ministers of the word; we are to "encourage *one another*". This applies to every one of us in our individual contact with each other, I have often been encouraged by simply meeting a brother in the street. A kindly word of interest and of cheer often goes a long way. A hearty grip of the hand is in itself an encouragement; when Paul says, "Greet one another with a holy kiss", he refers to the common salutation of the country, which answers to our shake of the hand. We might have thought a reference to such a thing beneath the dignity of Christianity, but not so the Holy Spirit. There are a thousand ways in which we can "encourage one another", if we are near the Lord ourselves.

And, remember this is to go on daily. We are not to be spasmodic. It is an easy thing to make a flash like a meteor, but if we are to be fixed stars shining with a steady light from day to day for the encouragement of others, we must ourselves daily abide in Christ, and walk in the Spirit. Then, instead of there being a falling off as to this, we should be encouraging one another, and *so much the more* as we see the day approaching (Hebrews 10:25).

May God write these things on our hearts, that we may be more distinctly FOR CHRIST as we wait for His coming! Amen.

———————

# THE NAZARITE'S VOW
## Numbers 6

Before entering upon the subject of the Nazarite's Vow I should like to say very plainly that the salvation of a sinner depends *altogether* upon Christ and His perfect work on the cross, and it is received *only by faith.* The prayers, works, self-denial, and devotedness of the believer add nothing whatever to his salvation. To suppose that our salvation depends in any way upon ourselves, is to be "fallen from grace", and to be in darkness and uncertainty as to the whole matter. But when we see that Christ is the Alpha and Omega of our salvation, that His atoning work has settled every question that sin had raised between God and our souls, that His blood cleanseth us from *all sin,* and that we are on the shoulders of the Good Shepherd who has pledged His word that we *"shall never perish",* we find ourselves upon solid ground, and divine assurance takes the place of alternating hope and fear.

An important fact is sometimes overlooked; viz., that salvation is linked with the recognition of the *rights of the Lord Jesus.* It is written, "If thou shalt confess with thy mouth the Lord Jesus, and shalt believe in thine heart that God hath raised him from the dead, thou shalt be saved", Romans 10:9. In a coming day *every* knee will be made to bow to Him, and *every* tongue will have to confess that Jesus Christ is Lord, but the believer does it now. By and by the rightful but now rejected King will have dominion from sea to sea, and from the river to the ends of the earth; but today His authority is only acknowledged and confessed by those who believe on His name. A little millennium is set up in the heart of the believer, and he confesses Jesus as Lord.

But sometimes Jesus is trusted as the Savior without being fully recognized as Lord. He is taken on board more as a Passenger than as Captain of the ship. The captain has authority from stem to stern; the ship sails whithersoever he "listeth"; everything about the vessel and her voyage is under his control. Now let each of us ask himself the question, Have I Christ on board as a Passenger or as Captain of the ship?

Some – Jacob-like – will give Christ the tenth part; others will offer Him a larger proportion; but giving Him one-tenth or nine-tenths is not really owning His rights. The inhabitants of a besieged city wanted to make terms with their enemies, but the answer was, 'No terms: *unconditional surrender*'. That is what we must have if we want to be Christians worthy of the name. No *terms* with Christ, but unconditional surrender to Him – the loyal and unreserved recognition of His rights as Lord!

And is He not worthy? Think of His unconditional surrender for us! See the Lord of glory stooping down into the dust of death! He sacrificed everything and laid down His life to make us His own. The love of Christ, expressed in death, has a constraining power over every heart that really knows it; and it argues with a cogency which nothing but the hardness of unbelief can resist, that we should not henceforth live unto ourselves but unto Him. Do we believe that *He gave Himself.* Then how can we make reserves in our surrender to Him? Shall we not fervently exclaim:

> *"Higher than the highest heavens,*
> *Deeper than the deepest sea,*
> *Lord, Thy love at last hath conquered,*
> *Grant me now my spirit's longing, –*
> *'None of self and all of Thee'".*

May all bargaining, and compromise and reserve, cease from our hearts here and now, and may that short but all-comprehensive prayer of a surrendered and subject heart – "Lord, what wilt Thou have me to do?" – be our soul's utterance tonight and evermore!

Surely none of us could be content to quietly assume that because our sins are forgiven we need not concern ourselves as to whether we are devoted to Christ or not! Let us not forget the judgment seat! Let us remember that there is such a thing as being "saved, yet so as by fire!" My brother, your present happiness and your future place in the kingdom of glory depend on your loyalty to Christ here on earth. May God touch us with a little of the fire that burned in the soul of a true Nazarite!

No one was compelled to be a Nazarite. The Lord wants a willing people now. The Nazarite was one who voluntarily devoted himself to the Lord – not of necessity but of a willing mind. *Grace* wrought in his heart the desire to be wholly for the Lord, and then grace provided a way in which that devotedness could be expressed. The great need of the Israel of God today is more Nazarites – more thoroughly devoted men and women. Spiritual *young men* are a great testimony for Christ in these days of secularised Christianity, and I should like every young man here to have it impressed upon his heart that God has committed to him a stewardship of the interests and glory of Christ. If we have not an intense longing to be really *for Christ* may God give it to us now!

Notice the three words – eight times repeated in this chapter:

"UNTO THE LORD".

These words are the key to the chapter. It is not "under the law", but "unto the Lord". There was no servile constraint – no legal bondage – about the Nazarite's vow. He was one whose heart burned with a desire to be wholly devoted "unto the Lord". Now I confess I know no arguments, and I am acquainted with no power, that will move the heart to devotedness except the knowledge of the Lord Himself and of His love. It is possible to read books by the score, and to listen to the most faithful and blessed ministry for years together, and yet never know the Lord as a present living Object in heavenly glory. I venture to say that it is impossible to see and know Him there by faith without having an intense desire to be wholly devoted to Him here. Do you think that we could gaze upon the glory-crowned Person to whom angels and principalities are subject, and yet withhold the allegiance of our poor hearts? Do you suppose for a moment that we could ponder the hands, the feet, the side, that bore the sufferings of His love to us, and remain in a state of passive indifference to

His glory here? Could we see Him there – the exalted Object of the worship of delighted heaven – and at the same time be content to compromise His glory and dishonor His Name by conformity to the world which still sets Him at naught.

A sight of that Man in the glory takes the glitter from this corrupt and Godless world. Its charms attract, and its shams deceive no more. The heart says, 'What have I to do any more with idols?' The One in glory becomes the "Object bright and fair, to fill and satisfy the heart", and the one who thus knows Him begins a new life. Instead of the affections and energies finding their home and object in the world and self, they begin to flow in the current of Numbers 6 – *"unto the Lord"*. It is not that we deny ourselves for an indefinite reason, or to improve our spiritual standing or reputation, but there is a positive Object – a Person of infinite worth – before our souls, and for the sake, and for the love, of that Person what would otherwise be painful self-denial becomes a source of deepest happiness to our souls. I am bold to say that the Nazarite who really devoted himself "unto the Lord" got overwhelmingly repaid for his self-denial in the blessing and joy of his soul. Now, my brethren, are you prepared to be true Nazarites! Does the Person of the Lord and

His love so command you, that the deepest and most cherished desire of your heart is to be devoted entirely to Him.

There were three things the Nazarite was not to do; these three negatives being simply the fruit and the expression of the positive fact that he was a man devoted "unto the Lord".

1. He was not to eat or drink any part, or product, of the vine.

2. He was not to cut his hair.

3. He was not to come in contact with a dead body.


1. The Nazarite willingly devoted himself to a life of

## SELF-DENIAL

and for the Lord's sake he abstained from that which would have been naturally pleasant to him. The testimony of Scripture is that "wine maketh merry" (Ecclesiastes 10:19), and "maketh glad the heart of man" (Psalm 104:15), and hence wine becomes the type of those earthly and worldly things that elevate and give pleasure to the heart and mind of man. The ordinary Israelite might indulge in wine and keep a good conscience; not so the Nazarite. The one who desired to be wholly for the Lord must abstain so totally that "from the kernels even to the husk" not a particle nor a drop that came from the vine of the earth must pass his lips.

Alas! my friends, there are thousands in the spiritual Israel today who are not Nazarites; professing Christians today are ready to drink every drop of the wine of earthly pleasure that they can get. They are ready to eat the whole vine – kernel, and husks, and all. The strait-laced legality of Puritan times has given place to a corrupt taste for pleasure and amusement, which is being gratified to the full by an unfaithful church, so that there is hardly any form of earthly or worldly pleasure which is not indulged in by professed people of God. My brethren, if you are set for the Lord, you will very soon find out that you cannot go to a cricket or football match, to a dramatic or musical entertainment, or to a worldly party, and that you cannot read light or fictitious literature, without defiling the head of your consecration. If you indulge in such things you will find that they destroy your interest in the things of God, they take away your liberty in prayer, they bring a shade upon your spiritual joy, and very soon – unless you repent – they will deprive you of all power to be a living witness for Christ.

I speak plainly because I do not believe that any of you want to be merely theoretical Christians. The things which I have mentioned carry so evidently the stamp of [he world upon them that you have probably shunned them ever since you were converted. Perhaps the girdle of truth needs to be drawn a little tighter than this around the loins of our minds. There are many things, which could not be pronounced sinful, from which a thoroughly devoted heart would hold itself aloof. Each of us has natural tastes and tendencies of thought which, if we had remained unconverted, would have dominated and colored our lives. With one it is a love for the society of friends, with another a taste for music, a third is held spell-bound under the magician's wand of the poet, the mind of a fourth is absorbed by mechanical or scientific ideas, and so on. Remember, I am not now speaking of what a man is engaged in as his business or profession, but of the source to which he turns for the pleasure of his heart when the claims of duty are discharged. Each of us, perhaps, could tell what he was naturally fond of, and each could perhaps also say that he had found by experience that the gratification of these natural tastes was not helpful to his spiritual life. All such things are products of the earthly vine – not always evil in themselves, but when the heart's affections are entwined round them, and the heart looks for its solace and joy in them, they have diverted us from the true source of our joy; they have displaced the Lord from His true place as our heart's absorbing Object, and the Nazarite is defiled.

A widow passing through a place where her husband had been murdered a few years before would hardly find much to gratify her heart there, however interesting the occupations, and however innocent and entertaining the amusements of the place might be! Now do we look upon this world as the place where the One we love best was murdered? The earth did not yield HIM wine, but vinegar and gall, and He – the true Nazarite – has turned His back upon all earthly joys, saying, "I will not drink of the fruit of the vine, until the kingdom of God shall come", Luke 22:18. His joys are with the Father and in heaven, and He would have us so to know and to share them that we might count it a gain to turn aside from the vine of the earth.

"Thy love is better than wine ... we will be glad and rejoice in thee, we will remember thy love more than wine", is the language of a heart truly attached to the Lord (Song of Songs 1:2 - 4); and David could say, "Thou hast put gladness in my heart, more than in the time that their corn and their wine increased", Psalm 4:7. Bear witness, every Christian heart! Have you not had seasons of joy in the Lord which have infinitely surpassed everything that the vines of earth can afford. Would you willingly and deliberately sacrifice the former for the sake of the latter? I think not. Then take heed that you are not beguiled by the serpent, who ever seeks to rob us of true joys by turning us aside to things which promise fair but which yield no real satisfaction to the heart! It is a real loss to us when we turn aside to these things, and we have to prove it so in the end; even as it is said of Israel, "My people have committed two evils; they have forsaken me, the fountain of living waters, and hewed them out cisterns, broken cisterns, that can hold no water". Jeremiah 2:13.

Deuteronomy 29:6 has been instructive to me in connection with this subject. "Ye have not eaten bread, neither have ye drunk wine or strong drink: that ye might know that I am the Lord your God". In the wilderness the Lord would make Himself the only Source, whether of sustenance or of joy, to His people. In the true spirit of this the altogether Perfect One refused both the bread (Luke 4:4) and the wine (Mark

15:23). He would only accept support from God. He would only have the solace and joy ministered by His God and Father. He was the true Nazarite. Even so He would have us to prove that He can carry us through this wilderness world without either its support or its solace. He would *make Himself our bread and our wine,* and, instead of being worse off, we should be infinitely better of, like Daniel's band, who were "fairer and fatter in flesh than all the children which did eat the portion of the king's meat". The devil is always ready to suggest that an out-and-out Christian is a melancholy creature, who does not enjoy life at all. Every thread of that suggestion, warp and woof, is a lie. I will show you directly what it is that makes the long faces and the sad hearts, but you may take it for granted in the meantime that it is not wholehearted separation to the Lord that makes a man unhappy.

Leviticus 10:9, 10, is another suggestive scripture as to this matter. "Do not drink wine nor strong drink ... that ye may put difference between holy and unholy, and between unclean and clean". A man cannot indulge in earthborn-joys without having his spiritual perceptions blunted. If he goes on with them he will presently tolerate what he would have once judged to be evil. Then godly watchfulness as to the little details of everyday life gives place to carelessness and laxity. Week by week the line of separation from the world becomes less distinct. Solidity and force of spiritual character is lost. The holy is not sought, nor the unholy shunned, with that intensity of purpose which once burned brightly in the soul; and ere long the once devoted saint drifts along with the circumstances by which he is surrounded, with little exercise and less joy, and completely shorn of the beauty of his Nazariteship.

Another solemn voice reaches us from Lamentations 4:7 - 8, "Her Nazarites were purer than snow, they were whiter than milk, they were more ruddy in body than rubies, their polishing was of sapphire: their visage is blacker than a coal; they are not known in the streets; their skin cleaveth to their bones; it is withered, it is become like a stick". How sad to think that the once lovely Nazarite may be reduced to such a condition as this! Have you never seen a blighted and withered Nazarite? – a man who has lost the simplicity that is in Christ, and the beauty of holiness, and all the devotedness and heavenly-mindedness that once shone so brightly in him? Now nobody can read Christ in him. His name may be on a church-roll somewhere; he attends meetings perhaps; but he is not known in the streets! The men where he works do not know that he is a Christian, and it is as well they do not, for he is now more like a spiritual scarecrow than anything else. A man in that condition, instead of attracting souls to Christ only scares them away. Let that man be a beacon-light to warn *you* from the rock on which he has made shipwreck! In ninety-nine cases out of a hundred the Nazarite's decline and fall *begins* by his turning aside to find pleasure in some joy that is of earth and not of heaven. The Lord loses for the moment His all-commanding and unrivalled place as the Object of the heart. This opens a crack – very small, probably, at first – but the devil has got wedges which are small enough *at one end* to get into the smallest crack; and when they are once in he knows how to drive them home, unless divine grace works repentance and restoration. Then you get a man like one of Jeremiah's Nazarites – worldly, conscience-smitten, and unhappy – a man who, sooner or later, will feel his thorough wretchedness; for if he is a converted man the Holy Spirit can neither give him the joys of heaven nor suffer him to be happy with the joys of earth. Thus, in seeking to enjoy two worlds he for the present loses both. Alas! poor man! may God make thee a warning to us all!

But the fearful results of a defiled

Nazariteship have also another voice to us! We should be not only constrained thereby to keep ourselves pure, but we should be also reminded of our responsibilities in regard to others. "I raised up ... of your young men for Nazarites ... but ye gave the Nazarites wine to drink", Amos 2:11, 12. I believe I am right in saying that the temptations which prevail most easily with the young in Christ are those which come from professing Christians. I have seen many a promising spiritual life blighted by the company and examples of professed believers. In this respect, "woe unto him that giveth his neighbor drink!" Remember the Savior's solemn words about an offence (or cause of stumbling) given to one of His little ones!

2. I think we may find a key to the significance of the unshorn locks of the Nazarite in a sentence from the apostle Paul – "Doth not even nature itself teach you, that, if a man have long hair, *it is a shame unto him*", 1 Corinthians 11:14. The Nazarite was found in a condition which, according to the thoughts of nature, was one of reproach and shame. In connection with this I should like to read Hebrews 11:24 - 26. "By faith Moses, when he was come to years, refused to be called the son of Pharaoh's daughter; choosing rather to suffer affliction with the people of God than to enjoy the pleasures of

sin for a season; esteeming

"THE REPROACH OF CHRIST"

greater riches than the treasures in Egypt: for he had respect unto the recompense of the reward". Here was a man most singularly favored by Providence as to his position in this world, who deliberately turned his back upon wealth, power, and honors, when all these things were within his grasp, and threw in his lot with people who were in circumstances of the lowest degradation! No doubt he made himself a laughing-stock for Egypt, but the laughing did not last very long, while the gain on the other side can never be calculated. To use the figure, Moses presented himself to Egypt with the unshorn locks of a true Nazariteship. He did not shrink from shame and reproach.

To "refuse" and to "choose" as Moses did, requires *uncompromising decision,* or what the New Testament calls "purpose of the heart". Jonathan's armor-bearer presents a fine example of a decided and devoted servant. "Do all that is in thine heart", said he to his master, "behold, I am with thee according to thine heart", 1 Samuel 14:7. He was thoroughly one with his master, regardless of consequences. It looked like tempting Providence, as people say, for two men to attack an army. Common sense would say, they will certainly be defeated, perhaps slain, or at any rate taken captive. The odds were fearful. The field of battle was a precipitous and unlikely place. Everything was against them. Nevertheless, he says, "I am with thee according to thy heart".

This is the spirit in which Moses acted. He recognized in the toiling brickmakers the chosen people of the Lord. If God's heart was with these poor toilers, Moses' heart would be with them too – not simply to pity and patronise them, but to suffer affliction, and bear reproach, along with them. No doubt people thought he was carrying things to extremes, and making a fool of himself. So he was, from Egypt's point of view, but he does not regret it today. We were singing just now

"Savior, I long to follow Thee,
Daily the cross to bear?"

When a man was seen bearing his cross, everybody knew that he had done with the world, and as long as he remained in it he was an object of contempt. Now is that what we covet and expect? It is all very well to talk and sing about it here in barracks, but how do we feel on the battle-field? We can all be very valiant for the truth when it costs us nothing. But a soldier must be prepared to stand fire, as well as to shine on the parade ground. It is at home, in the office, behind the counter, in the workshop, and on the street, in ten thousand details of everyday life, that the test comes. Are we prepared to face the Egyptians, and the Philistines, and all the foes of our Lord, ever saying to Him in loyalty of spirit, I am with thee according to thy heart?

Do we really look upon the sneers and scorn of the world as our greatest treasure upon earth? We are not told that Moses "submitted" to the reproach, or bore it well when it came, but that he *chose* it and esteemed it "*greater riches* than the treasures in Egypt". The spiritual millionaires are the men and women who have most of the reproach of Christ. In the coming day of kingdom glory I have no doubt many of the brightest crowns will be found upon the brows of people unknown to fame. Many an obscure saint has to face from morning to night the full, fierce tide of "the reproach of Christ". I have no doubt theirs will be a rich reward, while many a bit of showy service will be found in that day to have yielded "nothing but leaves".

There is another scripture which I dare say has already occurred to your minds in connection with this subject. "Let us go forth therefore unto Him without the camp, *bearing his reproach"*, Hebrews 13:13. This scripture appeals directly to the true Nazarite by the introduction of these two central words – "unto Him". But here a much narrower circle is in question. It is not now "Egypt", but "the camp"; i.e., the professed people of God. I cannot enter upon the subject now, but it would be easy to prove to you that the great religious bodies of Christendom occupy a position almost identical with the Jewish "camp" referred to here. In fact, much of the Christianity of today is only Judaism with Christian terms introduced into it; and there is as little true subjection to Christ and obedience to the will of God as there was in Israel when Moses pitched the tabernacle outside "the camp". The Nazarite would not be true to his consecration "unto the Lord" if he were to acquiesce in this kind of thing. Hence, he is called to "go forth therefore unto him *without the camp"*. But let him not suppose that his action will be either understood, or commended, by the "thousands of Israel!" He will be roundly abused by many; Pharisee and Bigot, will be the names hurled at him by some; while others will say that he is Peculiar, Narrow-minded, and, A man of very extreme views. In short, he must be prepared to carry his locks unshorn, and to bear "the reproach of Christ".

It is an evil day for the Nazarite when the questions begin to rise in his heart, Whatever, will they think? What will Mr. --- say? When he begins to consider the opinions of others, and to shape his course to please men, whether they be friends, or foes, the locks of his Nazariteship will soon be shorn. His spiritual strength will depart from him, and then woe be unto him when the Philistines come upon him!

A devoted Christian must be a fool in the eyes of the world and of carnal believers. He is impelled by unknown motives; he suffers loss with no visible compensation in any form; he goes calmly and steadily in the opposite direction to everybody else; he despises the advantages which all others are eager to pursue; he spends his time, his talents, and his means in the service and for the glory of One who is only a myth to men of the world. In a word, he lives "unto the Lord", and he is glad to be a fool *"for Christ's sake"*.

3. Finally the Nazarite was not, under any circumstances, to touch a dead body. In connection with this let us read Romans 8:12, 13. "Therefore, brethren, we are debtors, not to the flesh, to live after the flesh. For if ye live after the flesh, ye shall die: but if ye through the Spirit do mortify

the deeds of the body, ye shall live". Nothing could be more solemn than this scripture and its context, for it shows the absolute impossibility of *living to God* as men in the flesh.

The lesson learned by the painful exercises of Romans 7 is that "in me (that is, in my flesh) dwelleth *no good thing*", and the soul cries bitterly, "O wretched man that I am! who shall deliver me from *this body of death?*" The figure present to the writer's mind was that of the dreadful punishment of lashing a criminal to a dead body in such a way that it was impossible for him to free himself, and then leaving him to die. What was the dead body from which Paul had sought to be delivered? Was it not *himself,* and all that he was as a man in the flesh? Nor did he look for deliverance in vain! Having given himself up – as a man in the flesh – as being a "body of death", he looked outside himself for deliverance, and could immediately exclaim, "I thank God through Jesus Christ our Lord". He saw that the judgment of death had passed upon him at the cross, and that grace now gave him a perfect title to take the new ground that he was "in Christ Jesus". A door of life and liberty was thus opened to him, for "there is therefore now no condemnation to them which are in Christ Jesus" and, along with this, *power* by the Holy Spirit, so that he could say, "The law of the Spirit of life in Christ Jesus hath made me free from the law of sin and death".

Do not run away with the idea that I mean anything mystical or visionary when I say that the true Nazarite must live

## MORALLY APART FROM HIMSELF

as a man in the flesh. In saying this, I am speaking the sober and practical truth of the Scriptures, "If ye live after the flesh, ye shall die". "He that soweth to his flesh, shall of the flesh reap corruption", Galatians 6:8. You cannot come *morally* into contact with the flesh without being defiled. The Holy Spirit wages perpetual warfare against the flesh, and we are plainly told that if we walk in the Spirit, we shall not fulfil the lust of the flesh (Galatians 5:16). The Holy Spirit is dwelling in us to maintain us in freedom from that "law of sin and death" to which we were in bondage when we were "in the flesh". When a Christian thinks, or speaks, or acts, according to the flesh, he is practically acknowledging the man who is under death – the man who was set aside at the cross. To use the figure, he touches the dead body and defiles the head of his consecration. And, inasmuch as he is allowing that upon which death has passed in the sight of God, he has to reap from it death and corruption. We have to learn – it takes some of us a long time – that it does not pay to live after the flesh; to do so brings darkness into the soul, robs the heart of its divine joys, and entails the misery of an accusing conscience. Brethren, we cannot afford to embrace or cherish that "dead body" any longer. "They that are Christ's have crucified the flesh, with the affections and lusts", Galatians 5:24.

But if we refuse the vileness and wickedness of the flesh, let us not forget that the flesh has a moral and religious side which is equally defiling to the true Nazarite. We are often, like Saul (1 Samuel 15:9) ready to spare "the best" and the "good" of Amalek, while we would destroy utterly everything that is "vile and refuse". The Galatians, having begun in the Spirit, were seeking to be made perfect by the flesh. Some were insisting on the necessity for circumcision and keeping the law; they were observing days, months, times, and years; and were glorying in the flesh in a religious way. They were putting themselves again in moral contact with the "dead body" of the flesh, and Paul could hardly find language strong enough in which to describe their defilement thereby. He speaks of them as being "troubled", "bewitched", "foolish", turned away "to weak and beggarly elements, whereunto ye desire again to be in bondage", "fallen from grace".

The Colossians, too, needed to be warned against those who would spoil them "through philosophy and vain deceit, after the tradition of men, after the rudiments of the world, and not after Christ"; and they had to be asked, "Wherefore if ye be dead with Christ from the rudiments of the world, why, as though living in the world, are ye subject to ordinances?" Paul had to tell them that spiritual circumcision was the "putting off the body of the flesh by the circumcision of Christ". Christianity is not the flesh educated, or regulated, or decorated, but a new creation in Christ Jesus. If you see a man setting himself off with a religious title, or a religious dress, or even a bit of blue ribbon, you may be sure that he is not clear of the "dead body". He is not walking according to the rule of the new creation, but according to a rule which can be equally well carried out by an unconverted man. It seems a most admirable thing for a man to pledge himself to "Touch not, taste not, handle not" some evil thing; but the very fact that he puts himself under an ordinance as to it, shows that he is upon the old ground of a man in the flesh, on which ground he can never live unto God, or be a true Nazarite.

However fair it may promise, the flesh can never yield anything but defilement – death and corruption.

Then by what power can the spiritual Nazarite hold himself aloof from the "dead body" of his former self as a man in the flesh? Only by the Spirit of God. If we have not the Spirit, or if, having Him, we grieve Him, nothing can preserve us from living after the flesh. We naturally gravitate in that direction, and it is only as the counteracting "law of the Spirit of life in Christ Jesus" is in operation that we are maintained in freedom "from the law of sin and death". The spiritual Nazarite has no power to hold himself aloof from the "dead body", save as he walks in the Spirit. No words of mine can convey the importance and solemnity of this to your hearts, but I trust God will impress it upon us all. "Through the Spirit", and only thus, can we "mortify the deeds of the body", and keep ourselves morally clear of the flesh both in its carnal and legal aspects. There seems to be a great difference between flesh that is licentious and self-indulgent, and flesh that is exemplary, self-controlled, and ascetic. But flesh is flesh, and it is always opposed to what is of the Spirit of God. The better it looks, the more it is to be dreaded. In England the dissenting bodies have gone in for the cultivation of man's intellect as a chief part of preparation for the ministry. What is the result? Under cover of Higher Criticism, infidelity is now sown broadcast from many a pulpit from which a few years ago the truth of God was faithfully preached. On the other hand, the Establishment, under the influence of Puseyism, has laid itself out to cultivate the religious sentiment of the people. With what effect? Popery, in everything but the name, has spread itself over the land. Both have sown to the flesh, and of the flesh have they reaped corruption. Rationalism appeals to man as an intellectual being, and Ritualism appeals to him as a religious being. But both ignore the fact that "they that are in the flesh cannot please God"; both are clinging to the "dead body" which can only defile.

What happens on a large scale in Christendom is just what will happen in the smaller circle of our own lives if we do not walk in the Spirit, and as those who are alive unto God in Christ Jesus. May God keep us clear alike of the self-indulgence, the wisdom, and the religiousness of the flesh! May He keep us by His Spirit morally apart from that defiling "dead body"!

But what if the Nazarite be defiled? I think everyone present will be profoundly thankful to know that grace has anticipated the possibility of defilement, and has made provision for it. Yet let none of us overlook, or think lightly of, the solemnity of such a thing. Indeed, this scripture is one of peculiar impressiveness, in the solemn light which it throws upon the consequences of defilement. The brief hints which I can give you in the few moments that remain will, I trust, be followed up and searched out for yourselves.

The defiled Nazarite has, so to speak, to begin again. He shaves his head, and he brings a sin offering, a burnt offering, and a trespass offering to the Lord. When we defile the head of our consecration there is no restoration until God brings us back morally to the basis of all our blessing. The only ground, whether of our clearance from sin and judgment, or of our acceptance with God, is the death of Christ, and our hearts have to return to a sense of the infinite cost at which our clearance and acceptance have been secured. While this is in one way deeply blessed, and calls forth the full praise and worship of our hearts; it must, on the other hand, inevitably lead to the most profound self-judgment, as we are brought to see in God's presence that we have allowed that which Christ died to remove, and from the judgment of which nothing but His death could save us. Do you think it is a light matter to discover that we have allowed the very thing which cost the Son of God His life?

But there is another thing! "The days that were before *shall be lost,* because his separation was defiled". Is not this very solemn? The longer a Nazarite maintained his consecration, the more serious it was for him if he suffered himself to be defiled. I believe the longer we go on right, the more serious it is for us if we turn aside. We have to make it up *in moral time,* which is not reckoned in days, and months, and years, but *in exercise of soul.*

I trust that the Lord will set our hearts very distinctly for Himself, and that He will use what has come before us to warn us against the things that would defile the head of our consecration! It is worth our while to be out and out for Christ. There is not only "the recompense of the reward" by and by, but an immense return in spiritual blessing even now. It is at the end of this chapter – descriptive of a devoted man – that we find one of the most glorious benedictions that the Old Testament affords. "The Lord bless thee, and keep thee: the Lord make his face shine upon thee, and be gracious unto thee: the Lord lift up his countenance upon thee, and give thee peace". A devoted man is always a prosperous and happy man – of course, I mean spiritually. He honors the Lord with his substance, and with the first-fruits of all his increase, and the result is that his barns are filled with plenty, and his presses burst out with new wine. Your melancholy and long-faced Christians are not the out-and-out, but the half-and-half men – those who want to fear the Lord and serve their own graven images, to make the best of both worlds, or to be pious according to the flesh. They have never learned in their soul's experience the truth of Luther's definition of a Christian – that he is "a new man in a new world". At any rate, they are not practically owning that new man and living in that new world.

Numbers 5 tells us about the bitter water of jealousy and it ends with a curse upon the *unfaithful* one; but Numbers 6 describes one who is loyal to the core, and it ends with a blessing. It is even so with us. We are reaping governmentally day by day either the curse or the blessing. "Be not deceived; God is not mocked: for whatsoever a man soweth, that shall he also reap. For he that soweth to his flesh shalt of the flesh reap corruption; but he that soweth to the Spirit shall of the Spirit reap life everlasting".

———————

# "STAND FAST"

## 1 Corinthians 16:13; Galatians 5:1; Philippians 1:27; 4:1

We need to take it to heart, beloved brethren, that there is an immense power continually at work to move our souls away from the great fundamental realities of Christianity. All our natural tendencies are to drift away from what is of God. Hence, we have in the Holy Scriptures these repeated exhortations to *"Stand fast"*. Such exhortations would have no place or point if there was not a danger of our being moved away from our true position and the proper joy of our blessings.

I hope that no one here will think that I mean to say that a believer may be finally lost. The Lord's word has settled that. He has plainly said, "I give unto them [My sheep] eternal life; and *they shall never perish*". But in our Christian life and course on earth we shall lose our spiritual joy, the present purpose of God in saving us will not be carried out, His Spirit's work in us will be hindered and enfeebled, and consequently we shall be lean and poor in our souls, if we do not "stand fast".

## "STAND FAST IN THE FAITH"
## 1 Corinthians 16:13

It seems to me that at Corinth, where so many grievous things called for rebuke and correction from the Lord, the root of all the evil was that the believers there had failed to "stand fast in the faith". Neither the sectarian divisions, the legality, nor the carnality, which had come into that assembly, would have had a place there if the saints had been, in the power of the Spirit of God, standing fast in the faith.

I will read two portions from this epistle, to bring before you two prominent parts of the Christian faith. Of course, many other scriptures might be cited in connection with such an important subject, but these two will suffice for the present. "I delivered unto you first of all that which I also received, how that Christ died for our sins according to the scriptures; and that he was buried, and that he rose again the third day according to the scriptures", 1 Corinthians 15:3, 4. "But of him are ye in Christ Jesus, who of God is made unto us wisdom, and righteousness, and sanctification, and redemption: that, according as it is written, He that glorieth, let him glory in the Lord", 1 Corinthians 1:30, 31.

The first article in the Christian faith is that

"Christ died for our sins". Other scriptures tell us that He was delivered for our offences, that He bare our sins in His own body on the tree, that He by Himself purged our sins, entirely and eternally settling the question of our sins by His "one sacrifice". But *here* the fact on which special emphasis is laid is that "He died for our sins". It was necessary, in order to His bearing sins, that He should become a Man, and take part in flesh and blood. Though there was in Him no taint of sin and no liability to death, in perfect grace He took part in a life in which He could bear sins and be made sin for us – a life which He could lay down. He has fully glorified God about our sins, and has laid down the life in which He bore them. "Without *shedding of blood* is no remission". There is no removal of *sins apart from death*. The very life in which alone He could bear sins is ended; there is a complete removal of the whole thing. "Christ died for our sins".

And, further, He was buried, and rose again the third day. After bearing sins and dying for them He is risen from the dead. He lives now in a condition in which He can never bear sins, or come under death and judgment. After enduring and exhausting the full desert of our sins He has entered as the Risen One without spot into the unclouded light of God's presence, and God holds every believer to be as clear of sins as He is. This is justification. He was "raised again for our justification", Romans 4:25. There is a Man before God upon whom no spot can ever come, against whom no charge can ever be laid, a Man in unclouded and eternal acceptance, who is there as having dealt with and removed "our sins" to the perfect satisfaction of God. We are before God as clear of sins as He is. The knowledge of this gives cloudless and changeless peace. "Being justified by faith, we have peace with God through our lord Jesus Christ".

But the verses I have read from chapter 1 give us another and a most important part of the Christian faith. Many souls are not at perfect rest before God because they have not yet seen that Christ must be everything for them, and that it is only as being "IN Christ Jesus" that they can have any place in God's presence. Some believers that I know remind me of a dissolving view – one picture is beginning to fade and another is beginning to come, but for the present all is confused and indistinct. They have begun to distrust, and to be dissatisfied with themselves, but they have not yet altogether given themselves up. Christ has yet a certain place in the faith and the affections of their hearts, but they do not know what it is to be "in Christ Jesus", and to have Him as their "wisdom, and righteousness, and sanctification, and redemption". You will never have true Christian experience and joy until you learn in your soul that there is nothing about *you* – as in the flesh – but material for the judgment of God. YOU may think this is a hard saying, but I press it as the indispensable precursor of perfect rest and full joy in Christ.

There are two things which go to make up a man; i.e., wisdom and power. Deprive a man of these two things and he is reduced to a nonentity. Now if you read this chapter you will see that God has completely set aside man in the flesh as to both his wisdom and his power. See verses 17 - 29. No flesh can glory in His presence. And this is fully proved by the cross.

I see three things in the cross of Christ.

1. That man in the flesh has been fully exposed to the very roots of his moral being. The character of that man has come out perfectly. There were two great parts of God's claim upon man; first, that he should love the Lord his God with all his heart, soul, mind, and strength; and second, that he should love his neighbor as himself. It might have been possible in Old Testament times for men to say to God, 'We cannot love Thee, because we do not know Thee:

Thou has hidden Thyself in clouds and thick darkness'. But God has taken every argument of this kind out of man's mouth. He has sent His own beloved Son into the world to perfectly express His nature and character. What reception did He get? The world did not know Him, and His chosen people would not receive Him. Instead of loving God when He made Himself known, the cross was man's insulting answer to God's reconciling love.

Then as to man's duty to his neighbor. It might have been possible in Old Testament times for men to say, 'Our neighbors are all so imperfect that we cannot find one who is worthy of our love'. But this excuse will not answer now, for God has furnished man with a Neighbor in whom the most exacting scrutiny could not detect a flaw. Did man love his *perfect Neighbor?* Ah! no. Hear that fierce shout from frenzied throats – "Not this man, but Barabbas! Away with him! Crucify him!"

Man is fully exposed: he hates both God and his neighbor, when both are manifested in divine perfection. The cross is what the wisdom and power of man in the flesh led to, when he was allowed to take his own course. Could there be anything but judgment for such a creature?

2. I not only see man in the flesh fully exposed at the cross, but I see *that exposed man dealt with according to the holiness of God.* The One who hung upon that cross was there "for sin". He who knew no sin was there *made sin for us.* As I see Him drinking the cup from which every sensibility of His holy soul recoiled – as I hear Him cry, "My God, my God, why hast thou forsaken me?" – as I see Him brought into the dust of death – and know that it was *for me,* I have to own with an adoring heart that all that I am has been dealt with according to the holiness of God, and before God my history as in Adam has been closed in judgment and death.

3. There is a third thing, too, in that wondrous cross. I see there divine love bursting every barrier that man's sin had raised, that it might flow out and delight itself in the perfect blessing of its objects. By that cross the heart of God is righteously free to take its own wondrous course, and let out all its wealth of love upon sinners. The "river of God" can now flow out in floods of blessing, and in vast and widening streams of grace and glory through everlasting days. The old monk Suso might well say:

*"Wouldst thou know*
      *the wisdom and wonders,*
*Of God's everlasting plan?*
*Behold, on the cross of dishonour*
*A cursed and a dying Man!"*

The cross of Christ has closed our history before God as children of Adam, and God has now put us in a new position in Him who is raised from the dead. So that these words are true of all believers – "Of him are ye in Christ Jesus". No longer involved in the ruin and condemnation of Adam – no longer identified with the "flesh" which God cannot allow to glory in His presence – they are in the standing and acceptance of the One in whom every attribute of God finds its perfect satisfaction and its glorious display. This is the Christian faith!

Now, let me ask, what is the gain of being in Christ Jesus? In other words, what are the revenues of this new and exalted position? If the Queen gave some poor man a high position, everybody would expect her to furnish him with means to stand in that position with comfort to himself and credit to her. It is not less so with God, and when you take this new position you find that there are wonderful revenues connected with it. What vast stores of spiritual wealth are unfolded to our gaze in the words, "But of him are ye in Christ Jesus, who of God is made unto us wisdom, and righteousness, and sanctification, and redemption: that, according as it is written, He that glorieth, let him glory in the Lord".

I fear that many of us are like the Indian spy who received from George Washington, for services rendered during the American War, a parchment entitling him to a considerable pension. He hung it round his neck as a charm, and many years after, when he was dying in great poverty, it was found there – the written authority for him to have so many dollars a year until his death. He had never drawn a cent of the money, and though nobody could question his title to it, he had been no better off than if he had been without it. Would it not have been well for that man to have had some good friend to make him acquainted with the real value of his parchment, and to see that he got the good of it?

If we miss the enjoyment and use of the spiritual revenues to which we are entitled, it is not for want of a Friend to tell us what they are, or to see that we get the good of them. It is because we grieve that Friend, and hinder Him in all His efforts to help us. The Holy Spirit has been given to us, as the next chapter of this epistle tells us *"that we might know the things that are freely given to us of God"*, not simply that we might know about them, but know the things themselves.

Christ Jesus is of God made unto us *Wisdom*. The wisdom of men, or of this world, is no help to our souls. In some quarters it is considered essential that a Christian should be well read in "modern thought", and up to date in all the discoveries and speculations of science! God has said that He will destroy the wisdom of the wise, and will bring to nothing the understanding of the prudent; and that He has made foolish the wisdom of this world. See 1 Corinthians 1:19, 20, 27. The outlook of this world's wisdom is bounded by the grave. Death comes in, and in that very day man's thoughts perish. "There is no work, nor device, nor knowledge, nor wisdom, in the grave". That is, death deprives man of every single thing in which he can boast, or on which he can pride himself. Death strips man of everything but his responsibility to God, the full reality of which the unconverted man only then begins to know.

But the Christian anticipated all this. He sees the true character of man's wisdom, and recognizes that it must all wither under the blight of death; and he turns to

One who is risen from the dead, to find in Him the unfolding of divine thoughts, and wisdom of an imperishable order, connected with scenes where death can never come. The knowledge of God is true wisdom (see Proverbs 2:2 - 5) and while man is professing to seek after God, only to prove that by wisdom he cannot know Him, the Christian sees the light of the knowledge of the glory of God in the face of Jesus Christ.

Moreover Christ becomes the touchstone and test for everything. For example, there were some at Corinth who had drifted so far away from the faith as to say that there was no resurrection. This seemed to involve a peculiarly difficult subject, but spiritual wisdom brought in Christ, and the whole matter was settled at once. See 1 Corinthians 15:12, 20. Again, at Colosse the Christians were in danger of being drawn away by "philosophy and vain deceit, after the tradition of men, after the rudiments of the world". How does Paul expose the true character of all this? By adding, *"and not after Christ"*. That risen and glorified One is our Wisdom, and everything that is not of Him, or that turns us from Him, is folly.

Then there are often practical questions and difficulties in Christian life that call for wisdom. The true test and measure for everything is Christ. He is the true Solomon – the Solver of hard questions. It is astonishing how many perplexities disappear when our hearts are simple enough to bring in Christ. May we know more of what it is to have Him thus as our Wisdom!

Christ Jesus is of God made unto us *Righteousness.* How many are going about at this day, as of old, to establish their own righteousness! Some even who are truly converted are not free from legal thoughts as to this matter, and think that they must be, or do, something to improve, or maintain, their title to be in God's favor. My brother, if you had Elijah's faith, and Peter's fervency, and Paul's devotedness and energy, and John's love, you would not be one bit better off as to righteousness than you are now. We have a righteousness that is divinely perfect; we never did, and never could, contribute a fraction to it, and nothing can ever dim its brightness, or take from its excellence. "Not having mine own righteousness", says Paul, "which is of the law, but that which is through the faith of Christ, the righteousness which is of God by faith", Philippians 3:9. Now, my brethren, God would have our hearts to be maintained in the wonderful joy of this from day to day. I dare say most of us hold it as a doctrine, but to what extent are our hearts in the real good and present joy of the glorious fact that Christ Jesus is of God made unto us Righteousness?

Christ Jesus is of God made unto us *Sanctification.* No one truly knows what sanctification is until he learns this. A very common idea that people have of sanctification is that it consists of giving up things that one has a conscience about; i.e., things that are felt to be wrong. An unconverted man might do this, and there would be nothing of divine sanctification in it. But the moment we see that *a risen and glorified Man* is made unto us Sanctification, it carries us altogether away from the world and from what is of the flesh – *both bad and good.* Many a person would be quite happy to go to a Temperance Gala who would not think of going to a low Music Hall. But the one is as much of the flesh as the other, however great the difference may be morally and socially. Christ risen and glorified has nothing to do with either: He is outside everything that is of the world and of the flesh: He has sanctified Himself that we also might be sanctified through the truth. He is the measure of our sanctification, and the standard of our practical purification also; for it is written, "We know that, when he shall appear, we shall be like him; for we shall see him as he is. And every man that hath this hope in him *purifieth himself, even* as he is pure", 1 John 3:2, 3.

Christ Jesus is of God made unto us *redemption.* If we want to know what redemption is, according to God's thoughts, we must learn it in Christ Jesus. God makes Him the glorious Object Lesson, if I may so say, in whom we learn the divine fulness and perfectness of redemption. We see a man risen and ascended in a glorified spiritual body, and seated in unclouded acceptance at the right hand of God. He is the First-fruits of the resurrection harvest, in which the full display and triumph of redemption will be seen. He is the First-born among many brethren, who will all be conformed to His image in heavenly glory. Our salvation will not be entirely complete in result until He shall change our body of humiliation, and fashion it like unto His glorious body. *Redemption* in its full result and power cannot yet be seen in us; we are still in mortal bodies, and subject to disease and death. But Christ Jesus is of God made unto us redemption, and all that is true in Him, even as to bodily condition, will very shortly be true in us. His glory is the pledge and measure of ours.

Now, beloved brethren, are you living upon the revenues of your new position in Christ Jesus? God would have you to be supported and sustained by these things from day to day. The Holy Spirit dwells in you that you may know these things, and have the conscious enjoyment of them now. Whether as to wisdom, or righteousness, or sanctification, or redemption, are you finding *all* in Christ Jesus, and thus glorying in the Lord – rejoicing in Christ Jesus and having no confidence in the flesh? This is the Christian faith. The man after the flesh has gone, for God and for faith, and the Christian, by the Spirit, now finds everything in Christ Jesus – the Second Man. May we have grace in these evil days to "stand fast in the faith!"

## "STAND FAST ... IN THE LIBERTY".
### Galatians 5:1

The epistle to the Galatians is most solemn, because it shows how soon we may be drawn away from Christian liberty. The Galatians had heard a clear and full gospel from the apostle Paul, had been soundly converted to God, and had received the Holy Spirit. They had "begun in the Spirit", Galatians 3:3. I beg you to notice that expression. The man who is in the joy and blessing of the position and revenues we have spoken of in 1 Corinthians 1 is "in the Spirit". The Holy Spirit has brought him to renounce all confidence in the flesh, and has led him to find everything in Christ Jesus. The Galatians had known something of this, but had failed to "stand fast" in it, and it is most important that we should be warned against the beginnings of such an awful retrogression.

Mark the subtle way in which the enemy went to work in Galatia! We may imagine him speaking on this wise. 'Now you have made a good start, and have got wonderful blessings, and you will have to be very different men from what you have been in the past. You must now carry out all the word of God. Abraham and his descendants were circumcised by the command of God, and you must be so likewise. Then you may plainly see that God gave the law by Moses, and therefore that must be your rule of life. Further, you would be a better Christian if you were to fast once or twice a week; and at any rate you will observe the day on which your Savior was born, and that on which He died'. Thus the enemy and troubler of God's people speaks. Does it not sound very nice? Who would suspect any harm in such good words?

The fatal flaw in all this is that it turns the believer back to himself. It is all *you* must do this; *you* must do that; *you* must be thus; and so on. The mark of a man walking in the Spirit is that he is maintained in constant distrust of himself, and in constant satisfaction with Christ. We are then in happiness and liberty. But if Satan can succeed in turning us back to ourselves, though we may for a time think we are getting on splendidly and be very well satisfied with ourselves, the result will be darkness and bondage. The exhortation of Paul by the Spirit is, "Stand fast therefore in the liberty wherewith Christ hath made us free, and be not entangled again with the yoke of bondage".

In the old days of slavery, when a slave ran away from his master it was his great desire to reach British soil. On that ground, British law made him a free man. Our land of liberty is "in Christ Jesus", and the law of that land makes free; as Paul says, "The law of the Spirit of life in Christ Jesus hath made me free from the law of sin and death", Romans 8:2.

The Holy Spirit is indissolubly connected with "life in Christ Jesus". So that the Christian has not only a new *position* and new *revenues,* but also a new *Power* – a Power that acts to maintain him in the holy liberty of "life in Christ Jesus". I believe the first step on the way to weakness and bondage is to grieve the Spirit of God. If we do so we grieve the Person who is our only

Power, and the One by whom alone we can "stand fast" in the liberty. And does it not grieve Him when we turn back from Christ to be self-occupied and legal? It is going back to a man for whom God has nothing but judgment – a man whom He cannot support in any way.

There is real danger that those who have escaped to the free country may go back to the land of slavery. The Galatians had gone back. Well may Paul say, "O foolish Galatians, who hath bewitched you?" They did not know that in going back to the law and ordinances they were returning to man in the flesh, and glorying in flesh of which God had said that it should not "glory in his presence". They had got off the ground of being "IN CHRIST JESUS", and therefore had got out of touch with the Spirit of God, and were in legal bondage. Paul recalls them to their true position and privilege, and exhorts them to "stand fast" in it.

## "STAND FAST IN ONE SPIRIT,

with one mind striving together with the faith of the gospel", Philippians 1:27. The gospel was in great conflict; both Jews and heathen were opposed to it; but Paul was, as he tells us in verse 17, "set for the defense of the gospel". He was in prison for it *again,* as before at Philippi, and he was assured that the saints at Philippi were partakers of the grace that made him willing to be in prison for "the defense and confirmation of the gospel". See verse 7. He was not terrified but triumphant, and was anxious that the brethren should understand that the things which had happened to him had "fallen out rather unto the furtherance of the gospel" (verse 12); and he was willing either to live, or to die, for that holy cause. Now he longs that the Philippian saints should "stand fast" in this spirit, "striving together *with the faith of the gospel*" – that is, thoroughly identified with it in heart and interest – and in nothing terrified by their adversaries.

There is a danger of being selfishly occupied with our individual blessings, and forgetting that we are identified with a great and holy cause. The testimony and cause of God and of Christ is committed to us, and the maintenance of the whole depends upon each individual being true to his post. The strength of a British regiment depends upon every man that is in it, and every man feels in measure that he is responsible for the whole. Every man must stand heart to heart, and shoulder to shoulder; and it is something like that the apostle means when he says, "Stand fast in one spirit ... striving together with the faith of the gospel". It is not so much *preaching as suffering* that is in question here. Are we prepared to be true to divine colours whatever it costs us? It was prison for Paul. It was suffering for Christ's sake at Philippi. They were waging the same warfare in which they had seen the apostle engaged, and in which he was still suffering, see verses 29, 30. He was not terrified, and he did not want them to be so. He says, as it were, There is no fear; we are on the winning side; but let every man do his duty.

Humanly speaking, Paul had enough to dishearten him. He was in the hands of a bloodthirsty tyrant. The saints at Rome had turned their backs on him, and neither stood by him publicly, nor cared for his necessities privately. And yet he is as bold as a lion, and says, "I am set for the defence of the gospel". Is it not magnificent? He would face the combined power of the whole world single-handed for God's interests. True, he might be slain! Well, he had counted the cost, and it was his earnest expectation and hope that CHRIST should be magnified in his body *whether by life or by death.* God's cause might seem to be a hopeless one, but he was set for it. Like the noble captain of the *London,* who refused to save his life, but said, 'I will go down with the passengers', he would stick to his post, whatever it cost. Do we know anything of this spirit, my brethren?

You may say, and if you are like me you will say, 'I am such a poor weak thing I can do little or nothing'. It may be so, but do you bless God that He has called a poor heart like yours to the honour and joy of being identified with what He is doing for Christ in this world? There is no honour like it, and no favour from God so great as to be allowed "in the behalf of Christ, not only to believe on him, but also to suffer for his sake". It is not so much the outward service of the hands, and feet, and lips, though this is important in its place, but the loyal spirit of hearts that seek not their own things, but the things which are Jesus Christ's.

### "STAND FAST IN THE LORD"
### Philippians 41

In saying this, Paul was not telling them to do something that he knew nothing of himself. He says, "*I trust in the Lord* that I also myself shall come shortly", Philippians 2:24. He had no human reason to expect that he would see them again, but when he looked at it in connection with the Lord, he had faith that he would see them. When the Lord is brought in what are all the powers either of Jerusalem, or of Rome? Then the Philippians were to receive Epaphroditus "in the Lord" (verse 29); he had gone through a most trying service to bring their gift to Paul, and now he was coming back, and was to be received – not merely in the way of human friendship – but "in the Lord". Further, the apostle says, *"Rejoice in the Lord ... Rejoice in the Lord alway";* (chapter 1: 3-4) – not in circumstances, however bright, but in the Lord. If circumstances were dark the joy would not suffer if it was "in the Lord". Again he says, when receiving the help they sent him, he *"rejoiced in the Lord* greatly", chapter 4: 10. In every circumstance, and at every moment, the Lord was the first Person before his heart. He was looking at everything, and holding everything, in connection with the Lord. I think that is standing fast in the Lord.

If we were thus standing fast in the Lord do you not think it would often make a great difference? Perhaps half of our lives would have to drop out of existence, and the other half be strangely altered! Everything that could not be connected with THE LORD would have to go, if we were truly standing fast in the Lord.

It seems that two sisters at Philippi had some little difference. How does Paul put them right? "I beseech Euodia, and beseech Syntyche, that they be of the same mind *in the Lord*", chapter 4:2. If things were not right between you and me, and both of us were to get into the presence of the Lord, and give Him His right place in our hearts, we should be of one mind. Not simply one giving in to the other, but both giving in to the Lord. Have you never fancied that you had some great grievance, and got so under it that you felt you must go to the Lord about it? It was a mountain when you began, but somehow as you told Him about it, it grew less and less, until at last you were heartily ashamed that you had ever mentioned it to Him, or allowed it a place in your heart?

May the affectionate words of the beloved apostle be treasured, and heeded, in all our hearts! "Therefore, my brethren dearly beloved and longed for, my joy and crown, so stand fast in the Lord, my dearly beloved".

---

# THE LOST HOPE

The promise of John 14:3, is on the eve of being fulfilled; the threefold summons of 1 Thessalonians 4:16 will soon be heard; the wise and foolish virgins of Matthew 25 are about to be eternally separated: in short, *the Lord Jesus Christ is coming again.*

That promise, first falling from His own lips in John 14, formed the substance of a special revelation given to Paul (1 Thessalonians 4:15), and was thrice repeated in the *last* message which a glorified Christ sent down to His waiting Bride. Revelation 22:7, 12, 20.

The Lord did not intend these words to be an empty sound, devoid of meaning, power, or effect upon the hearts of His loved ones; they were uttered to kindle there a responsive flame of joyous expectation. And this *was* the effect upon the hearts of the early believers. The Lord's return was to them a "blessed hope". It was no visionary prospect, but a reality which commanded their affections and could be seen expressed in their everyday lives. They waited "for the coming of our Lord Jesus Christ" (1

Corinthians 1:7); they waited for God's "Son from heaven" (1 Thessalonians 1:10); they "went forth to meet the Bridegroom".

It was this that made them practically a heavenly people. Links with earth were broken; connections with the world were severed. Earth's wealth and splendor, its gilded attractions, all its bewitching sorceries, have lost their charm and power over a man who knows the Lord Jesus Christ as his Savior, and who is continually expecting that Savior's voice to translate him in a moment to endless glory. He is so dazzled by the bright visions which pass before 'faith's transpiercing eye', that this world's glory seems dull and dim. So, the early Christians were a separate and an unworldly people. Their hearts had been touched by a Savior's love; they knew that His precious blood had washed away all their sins, and their whole souls were fired by the expectation of seeing His face and being with Him and like Him forever.

The language of their hearts was –

*"Oh, worldly pomp and glory!*
*Your charms are spread in vain!*
*I've heard a sweeter story,*
*I've found a truer gain.*
*Where Christ a place prepareth,*
*There is my loved abode!*
*There shall I gaze on Jesus;*
*There shall I dwell with God!"*

Their heavenly mindedness drew down upon them the scorn, contempt, and violence of men. By their separation from the world they testified against it that its deeds were evil, and the world hated, despised, and rejected them, thus affording them the high honor of fellowship with their adorable Master. They could afford to "take it patiently" knowing that His coming drew nigh (James 5:7, S), when His own approving smile would more than compensate for all the contradiction of sinners they had to endure. Ah! the Lord's coming was not to *them* a doctrine, or a theory, but a hope of strengthening, sanctifying, transforming power.

Satan sought by every means to quench their testimony. The fiery sword of persecution was unsheathed against them with relentless severity, until Satan found that the blood of the martyrs was the seed of the church, and "the more they afflicted them, the more they multiplied and grew".

So, when violence failed he tried corruption, and began to seduce the church by offering her the very things which Jesus had refused – the world and its glory.

Would she have them? Would she accept flattery and aggrandizement, at the hands of the world, those very hands which were stained with the blood of her rejected and murdered Lord? Alas! she forsook her first love. She laid aside the gory crown of martyrdom and assumed the glittering tiara of earthly grandeur and supremacy. As the world crept in, the hope of the Lord's return died out. That hope which had burnt with such a vehement and ardent flame gradually grew dim. The heart ceased to long for Him; the eye ceased to watch for Him. Solemn words, *"While the Bridegroom tarried, they all slumbered and slept"*. A worldly church could not cherish the prospect of the Lord's return. At the same time the glorious truths of eternal redemption, the present forgiveness and justification of all believers and their possession of eternal life in the knowledge of the true God and Jesus Christ, His sent One, were obscured, perverted, or denied; so that all certainty and assurance was taken even from those who were really the children of God; and the thought of the Lord's coming became a terror for the conscience rather than a delight for the heart.

The Lord's coming was referred to the end of the world, and invested with ideas of terror and judgment, which plainly proves that the church had sunk down to the level of the world. The world's guilty conscience can only predict a day of certain judgment if Jesus comes again. But *believers* know, or ought to know, that there is no judgment for them (John 5:24); Jesus has borne their sins at His first coming, and has whispered the wonderful love-secret into their ears that He is coming again to receive them unto Himself, that where He is there they may be also. He is coming for us not as a Judge, but as a Bridegroom – coming that He may have us where every affection of His blessed heart can flow out unhinderedly upon us. How strangely sad that such a hope should have been lost! Yet so it was for more than fifteen hundred years.

Theologians wrote of the Lord's coming; it is true; but how did they write? They wrote of His appearing as the Judge of quick and dead; of His solemn session on the Great White Throne; of His dividing the sheep from the goats; and they spoke of that day as being the time when we should know whether we were saved or not; for they had not the present knowledge of forgiveness or salvation which God gives in His word to all believers. See John 5:24; Acts 13:38, 39;

Colossians 1:12 - 14.

Jesus will appear as the Judge and every eye shall see Him; but this is not the character of His coming for believers. Before He comes as the Judge to the world, He will come as the Bridegroom to call away His saints. Hence, we find that when He appears publicly in glory and power, His saints appear *with* Him. Colossians 3:4; Jude 14; Revelation 19:8-14. His coming as the Bridegroom is the Hope of the church, and this was lost sight of when the church became worldly in the time of Constantine; and all through the dark ages of papal supremacy, and even in the brighter days of the Reformation, it was never recovered, and might truly be called

### THE LOST HOPE

A little over a century ago, God was pleased to restore many precious truths from the obscurity into which they had been driven. Amongst others, the full present knowledge and enjoyment of the forgiveness of sins, and the possession of eternal life, were seen to be the portion of every believer on the Lord Jesus Christ. The perfection of the atoning work of the Son of God in clearing all believers from all their sins was apprehended more fully than before. The fact that believers are seen of God as dead and risen with Christ, and now by the Holy Spirit have power to *reckon themselves* dead indeed unto sin, was discovered to be the secret of liberty, and of a holy life. It was also seen that believers are indwelt by the Holy Spirit, and thus united to Christ in glory as the members of His body; then shone forth again that blessed Star of hope which had been hidden so long by clouds of worldliness and unbelief. THE lost hope began to burn again in a few loyal and devoted hearts. The midnight cry began to ring out – "Behold the Bridegroom; go ye out to meet him".

It was at once felt that conformity to the world's fashions, customs, and conversation was inconsistent with the hope; in fact, as it was cherished it exerted its purifying effects (1 John 3:3) upon the hearts and lives of those who had it, and they were marked by separation from the world, by simplicity in life, and by godliness in conversation. Their watchword seemed to be "Let us watch and be sober". They were a holy, happy, heavenly people.

Years passed on. From those in whose hearts the cry first sounded it went forth to a sleeping church. What numbers of slumbering ones were aroused by that cry! What a trimming of lamps; what a girding of loins ensued! Thousands will have cause to bless God throughout eternity that it reached their cars. Professors who had but an empty lamp, were led to obtain a supply of the precious oil of which they were destitute; doubting believers to rest in the finished work of Christ, and to rejoice in a known and accomplished salvation; and many dear saints of God saw new glories in Christ as the Head of His body, the Church. God was preparing the way for the return of His Son.

Yes, a hundred years and more are passed, and that "blessed hope" remains unfulfilled. The Lord is still seated on His Father's throne, and His people await the moment of His rising and descent into the air. Precious and true as ever is His closing word – "Surely I come quickly!" and He looks for the fitting response – "Even so, come Lord Jesus".

Can it be untimely or inappropriate to ask, is this the present attitude of His bride? Alas! even yet many saints are actually ignorant of the fact that "the coming of the Lord draweth nigh"; while the scoffer asks boldly, "Where is the promise of his coming?" On the other hand, multitudes in Christendom have heard that Jesus is coming, and have been convinced from Scripture of the truth of the doctrine. Some have heard that midnight cry, and it has had the effect of causing them to go forth "to meet him"; hence, for more than a century small companies of believers have gathered to His name, to remember Him who was once offered to bear their sins, and who will appear the second time, apart from the question of sin, to effect the salvation of the body; to these latter a few words are now addressed.

Are you, beloved, waiting and watching? Is such the character which is expressed by your lives? Very loth should we be to give up the *doctrine* of the Lord's coming, but do we know the reality of it as a hope? Let the truth be faced and owned. Do our words, our ways, our surroundings bear testimony to our profession that we have "turned to God from idols to serve the living and true God; and to wait for his Son from heaven"? Does He who reads our hearts and discerns our secret thoughts know that we dearly cherish this precious truth, possess in power this blessed hope, and day by day eagerly await its fulfilment? Must we not confess that in many cases where the *truth* of the Lord's coming is held, it fails to detach the heart from the world, to separate it from earthly things, and connect it with brighter things above? Surely in such cases, though the truth is held,

## THE HOPE IS LOST.

For aught we know, the Lord may come today. If so, in what state will He find us?

With what are our hearts taken up, and on what subjects are our tongues moving? The Lord Himself? His unchanging love? His speedy return? The Lord grant that we may be in a state

> *"Like that which was found*
> *in His people of old,*
> *Who tasted His love,*
> *and whose hearts were on fire*
> *While they waited, in patience,*
> *His face to behold".*

And what was the spiritual state of that "people of old" – the Simeons and Annas of that day? The Spirit of God tells us (Luke 2) that they were "just and devout"; serving God "with fastings and prayers night and day"; speaking "*of HIM to all them* that looked for redemption in Jerusalem"; men and women in the power and current of the Holy Spirit.

Oh! saints of God, what course can we adopt other than to bow low before Him, and own that we have lost the reality and freshness of "that blessed hope"; that we have allowed the things of earth to enter our hearts, and frustrate its separating power; meanwhile praying that in His great mercy He will revive again in our hearts, and restore in sanctifying power to our souls, this most precious hope? Nor let us forget that cheering word – "Blessed are those servants, whom the Lord, when he cometh shall find watching: verily I say unto you, that he shall gird himself, and make them to sit down to meat, and will come forth and serve them".

Oh! beloved saints, let us awake to the fact that He is just about to return! let us re-trim our lamps, if need be, again and again; let us "be filled with the Spirit", that we may possess, enjoy, and exhibit the effects of this hope in living power; meanwhile seeking, in the power of the same Spirit, to "occupy" till He come.

———————

www.ingramcontent.com/pod-product-compliance
Lightning Source LLC
LaVergne TN
LVHW051632080426
835511LV00016B/2302